ad usum
M J Kennedy Cm
22 april 99

Images of Mary

Brother Joseph Aspell, S.M.
SEAT OF WISDOM
1995
Bronze, life-size sculpture in
Saint Elizabeth Seton Church, Orland Hills, Illinois

IMAGES OF MARY

❊

Alfred McBride, O. Praem.

ST. ANTHONY MESSENGER PRESS

Cincinnati, Ohio

Cover painting by Darina Gladišová, *Blue Madonna*,
copyright ©1998
Cover design by Sanger and Eby Design
Electronic pagination and format design by Sandy L. Digman

ISBN 0-86716-330-5

Published by St. Anthony Messenger Press
Printed in the U.S.A.

CONTENTS

PREFACE

The woman loved autumn afternoons. The quieter
sun rested more peacefully on the toast-colored
stones of her home. A lone eagle floated in the
cloudless sky. This was intermission time in her
small village—the pause between siesta and the
companionable noises of supper preparation. She
found a center of inner peace and stayed there,
until...

The purposeful young man had been searching
for her. The old village had several winding streets
that misled him, until he finally found her. He could
tell he was intruding somehow, but he wanted to
meet her. He felt awkward, somewhere between his
impulsive nature and innate sense of respect.

His name was John and he had recently become
a follower of Jesus. He needed to know what the
woman was like. He sat on the ground before her
and took the hem of her cloak and kissed it.

"You are his mother."

The woman remembered. She was good at that.
She had a way of storing memories. She saw the
scene again, the noisy and curious visitors who
wanted to look at her, the glib praise and the
startling response. She made it a memory and
polished its beauty. To this eager young man she
said:

"Those who hear the word of God and keep
it.... They are his mother" (cf. Luke 8:21 and Mark
3:34-35).

I have adapted this brief scene from Franco Zeferelli's television film, *Jesus of Nazareth*, for two reasons. First, because he has taken a Gospel quote about Mary and given it a twist that makes it come alive again. Second, because it is a way of saying that Mary was her Son's first disciple. When Jesus spoke those words, he knew that Mary understood best how to hear God's word and keep it.

Discipleship is one of ten images we will explore in this book. Catholics are very fond of Mary and, like all lovers, each Catholic has a favorite image. Today, millions of Catholics are drawn to Mary of the Appearances and the graces of her apparitions. But in other ages, believers have lovingly focused on a variety of Mary's gifts.

Second-century Christians venerated her as the New Eve. Then, with the rise of an attraction to consecrated virginity, they sang to Mary Ever a Virgin. In 431, when the Council of Ephesus declared Mary to be Theotokos—the Mother of God—enthusiastic believers coursed through the city in the first recorded Marian procession, chanting hymns and carrying candles and praising God for this singular honor given to her.

If our faith ever needed a poet to celebrate Mary, we found the best man in Saint Bernard, whose *Missus Est* sermons brought the mystery of the Annunciation unforgettably to our attention. Here he gave us the image of a woman who made the most consequential decision in history, her "yes" to the Incarnation. The Annunciation may well be the most painted scene in Western art.

A countercultural Church has found in Mary exactly the right response to a world much too insistent about the imagined irrelevance of religion. The nineteenth century flexed its humanistic muscles and created the myth of progress, arguing that human nature can shrug off the "fable" of original sin. Marxist man can create a workers' paradise. Darwin's evolving humans can change the world by their own power. John Locke's leviathan super-state can solve all economic and political problems.

In the middle of all this stress on human potential and denial of sinfulness, the Church placed before the world the image of the Immaculate Conception. It was a daring and unpopular decision. Protestants dismissed the event as outmoded and outrageous. Secular culture laughed at what it considered a quaint throwback to medievalism.

Yet the Spirit wisely moved the Church to affirm the doctrine of Mary's preservation from original sin based on the anticipated merits of Christ's redemptive act. The culture said we were original blessings—"noble savages" in the words of Rousseau—and intrinsically good. We can trust the humanness of human nature. The Church replied that human nature is good, but basically flawed. We need redemption just as Mary did. We need continuous graces to help our human acts to achieve goodness, justice and fulfillment. Inevitable progress is not a certainty.

In the twentieth century the myth of progress exploded. We have seen the worst wars and greatest slaughters in history. The cruelty has been unimaginable. In future ages, the death camps will be the shameful icons of this century. Fashionable pessimism has replaced naive optimism. Despair has infected the culture. This was especially true in mid-century just after the second of the great wars.

Again the Church turned to Mary to reverse the culture's newest waywardness. In 1950, Pius XII proclaimed the dogma of Mary's Assumption. Just when the world was depressed by the degrading of tens of millions of human bodies, scattered on battlefields, beaten and gassed in death camps, burned by the bombs of Dresden, London and Hiroshima, the Church offered people the glorious image of the body of Mary taken into the perfection, love and honor of heaven.

Exactly when the memory of the killing fields was most fresh, the Church said, "Look at Mary's body clothed with the sun, crowned with stars, honored and exalted by Father, Son and Spirit." It was not just a question of the flesh, but of the dignity of the human person and the enduring grounds for hope that the mystery reveals.

It is my intention in this book to lay before you the tapestry of Mary's images from New Testament times to the present. While we probably cannot avoid having our favorite image, we will be wise to adopt the "principle of totality" which gives us the whole mosaic comprised of our images of Mary. For this purpose I have included the background for each image, grounded in Church history, wherever necessary. This healthy approach will deepen our faith, guarding us from extremes and broadening our ecclesial outlook. It will protect us from a narrow theology of scarcity and liberate us for a theology of abundance. I think it will become clear that we contemplate Mary because she mirrors Christ and the Church.

In the first four centuries of Christianity, the Church Fathers found in Mary essential clues about Christ that helped them turn back the heresies of Gnosticism (Jesus isn't human) and Arianism (Jesus isn't divine). In our own day, the Fathers of Vatican II placed their chapter on Mary in the Dogmatic Constitution on the Church (*Lumen Gentium*). When they wanted to illustrate the virtues of the Church, they held up Mary as a model. When they desired to help us grow in discipleship, they asked us to look at Mary.

When Paul VI searched for a contemporary image of Mary that seemed to suit our times best, he selected the title Mother of the Church. As you will see in my final chapter, Pope John Paul II gathered up the implications of this image in his inspiring encyclical, "Mother of the Redeemer," and wrote one of his most lyrical passages about it. I do not recall ever reading a more profound interpretation of Christ's words, applying "Woman, behold, your son," to her motherhood of the Church.

I have enjoyed writing this book for many reasons, not the least of which is my love for our Blessed Mother. Like any loving son, I want to do the best for my mother. When I see other tributes to Mary—what the architects of the great cathedrals have erected and what splendid canvases artists have painted and what poems the poets have composed and what profound treatises theologians have written—I consider my words to be a modest contribution at best. Still, when something is done for love is this not enough?

I have shared here my love of the Virgin Mary with you. If you catch any of it, will you share it with others? She had the face that most resembled Christ's. She wants to be your mother; if I have succeeded in helping you know that, I will have achieved my purpose.

Feast of the Assumption, 1997

Novgorod School
THE ASCENSION OF OUR LORD
1543
Russian icon from the Malo-Kirillov Monastery
Museum of Art, Novgorod, Russia

CHAPTER ONE

❊

The Mystery of Mary

You, Jesus, and your mother alone

are beautiful in every way.

In you no stain,

in your mother no spot.

— *Saint Ephrem of Syria*

Protected From the Rain

My mother died when I was a senior in high school and one of her wishes for growing older was to see me graduate from college. Being the youngest of eight, I figured she would always be around and I would tell her she would see me married with kids. Sadly none of that came to pass, at least not physically. I know my mother was with me at my high school graduation and I feel her with me and my family today. I also know she was watching the day I graduated from Notre Dame by a sign I received at the Grotto [of Our Lady].

On the way to the graduation at the Joyce Center I stopped by the Grotto to say a prayer of thanks and to light a candle for my mother. There I was clad in my cap and gown on a sunny, hot and humid May 16. As I knelt and said my prayers the thunder clouds began to roll in and just as I began to light the candle, the skies opened up and the rain came pouring down. Five minutes I watched the rain fall and prayed to my mother thanking her for all she had done and wishing that she was there, all the while I was safe and dry in the haven we call the [G]rotto. Some would say it was luck; a meteorologist would say it was natural, but that rain stopped just in time for me to make it to graduation and there were a lot of wet graduates who weren't so lucky to be in a safe and dry place....

No visit to the campus is complete without a visit to the Grotto. I visited it often when an undergrad, but since it has been five years since my last visit, I wish I had stopped by more.

— *Brian J. Fogarty,* from Grotto Stories: From the Heart of Notre Dame

I hope you found Brian Fogarty's memory of the Grotto at the University of Notre Dame as appealing as I did. His story is part of a collection of such anecdotes from Notre Dame alumni and friends. I was given a copy of the book by Sister Lourdes Sheehan who was running the Alliance for Catholic Education on the campus in the early nineties.

The cumulative impression I received from the stories was the simplicity of faith of the students and their trust in Mary as a key part of their spiritual lives.

They all considered the Grotto the "heart" of Notre Dame. That was remarkable because the competition from the excitement of football weekends is formidable. Equally compelling is the vast enterprise of higher education and intellectual pursuits. Yet they said the heart of the campus was the shrine of the Mother. This in no way detracts from sports or learning. Mary is the spiritual mother of the whole person.

My earliest memories of the Blessed Mother go back to sodality devotions on Thursday evenings in Philadelphia. During my early childhood, my mother brought me with her to these services. They included some Marian hymns, the recitation of several psalms, the Litany of Loretto and Benediction of the Blessed Sacrament.

Generally there was no variation. The repetition of the same psalms, hymns and prayers had a soothing effect, creating a familiarity with Mary and a homelike mood. The only change in those years was the building of a replica of the Lourdes grotto, with its sea of candles, an earnest, kneeling Bernadette and the graceful image of Mary as the Immaculate Conception.

Our closing hymn was always "Immaculate Mary." Mary became very real for me in those impressionable years. I had no difficulty conversing with her, not at any great length, mind you, but enough to stay in touch. She was then, and is now, that patient "waiting mother" who keeps pulling me back to Christ and the Church.

There was an intensity of affection for Mary among the people I knew in the thirties and forties. World War II began during my teen years and parents were worried about the safety of their children involved in the war effort. Our pastor, Father James Vallely, introduced the Miraculous Medal novena on Sunday nights to pray for peace and protection. The great upper church of St. Patrick's was filled with over a thousand people for every service. Instinctively, parents felt Mary would look out for their children. The walls rang with a thousand voices singing of Mary, "Star of the Sea"—a beloved image borrowed from Italian sailors who had entrusted themselves to Mary for centuries.

Today again I live amid a wave of Marian devotion. Though some Protestants and many Moslems honor Mary, it's a distinctively Catholic thing among Western Christians, isn't it? Well, what's going on? Why is it happening? Let's look at the present development.

When the Holy Spirit touched the womb of Mary two thousand years ago, a prediction arose from the lips of the Virgin, "All generations will call me blessed." She was more right than she might have imagined. Mary of Nazareth, the mother of Jesus Christ, is the most celebrated and venerated woman in all of history.

And attention to Mary is more pronounced than ever.

Every day, the faithful recite two billion Hail Marys. Last year alone, five million pilgrims journeyed to Lourdes in France and ten million went to Guadalupe in Mexico. Millions more went to Fatima, Czestochowa, Medjugorje and American sites such as Emmitsburg, Maryland, and the National Shrine of the Immaculate Conception in Washington, D.C.

More girls are named for Mary than after any other historical figure. New books about Mary appear regularly, such as *Mary Through the Centuries* by Yale professor (and Lutheran) Jaroslav Pelikan. Feminist writers, such as Oxford historian Marina Warner, author of *Alone of All Her Sex*, have been attracted by the meaning of Mary for the modern woman. Even the Koran praises her chastity and faith.

Artists, composers, sculptors, poets and architects have produced paintings, hymns, statues, poems and cathedrals honoring Mary in such abundance that no other person, save Christ, comes close.

Surprisingly, even popular journalism has discovered Mary. *Time* magazine chose Mary for its Christmas cover story in 1991 and *Life* picked her for its Christmas cover story in 1996.

Marian devotion waxes and wanes, often in response to the social and religious climate. After Vatican II, there was a notable decline. Ecumenical dialogue with Protestants uneasy about the Catholic emphasis on Mary tended to leave her out of the conversation. And a few small, cautionary sentences in Vatican II's pronouncements caused many to abandon Marian devotion—and Catholic devotional practices in general:

> [The Council] strongly urges theologians and preachers of the Word of God to be careful to refrain as much from all false exaggeration as from too summary an attitude in considering the special dignity of the Mother of God....
>
> Let them carefully refrain from whatever might by word or deed lead the separated brethren or any others whatsoever into error about the true doctrine of the Church. Let the faithful remember moreover that true devotion consists neither in sterile or transitory affection, nor in a certain vain credulity....
> — *"The Church"*

The Church has always distinguished the adoration due to God from the veneration due to Mary: We adore God; we honor Mary. Since this distinction is sometimes lost on non-Catholics, the Council issued the above statement in the hope of abolishing *excess*, not the legitimate and ancient veneration due to Mary. But such admonitions, important and necessary as they were, had the unintended consequence of casting a shadow over Marian piety, eroding her place in the Catholic consciousness.

The election of Pope John Paul II in 1978 signaled a turnaround for the revival of interest in Mary. He chose as his papal motto, "Totus Tuus" (Totally Yours), an expression taken from Saint Louis de Montfort's prayerful seventeenth-century classic, *True Devotion to Mary*. To the dismay of purists, who argue no writing should appear on a coat of arms, the pope put the letter *M* (for "Mary") on his crest. To the joy of Marians, John Paul II never missed an opportunity to visit a Marian shrine during his many pastoral visits around the world.

Coupled with this is an explosion of reported Marian apparitions—from the former Yugoslavia to Colorado, from Cairo to Caracas. While it is too early for the Church to determine whether any of these deserves official approval, believers, skeptics and the curious flock to the sites.

One such site, Medjugorje, in the former Yugoslavia, has had an enormous impact all by itself. Hundreds of Medjugorje groups exist across the United States. They publish thirty newsletters and sponsor a dozen conferences a year. A Texas foundation has mounted 6,500 billboards inspired by Medjugorje. Thousands testify to the experiences they have had at the site, inspiring them to make radical changes in their life-styles.

Grass-roots devotion to Mary has never been greater. Yet, paradoxically, there is very little about Mary in Scripture—all the scenes about Mary in the New Testament put together scarcely fill a few pages. So what is behind all the excitement? What is there about the mystery of Mary that inspires such a global outpouring of attraction to her?

Three reasons come to mind.

Theological Principle

First, the Church has established a theological principle that connects Mary to Christ and the Church. We look at Mary to understand Jesus and the Church more clearly. Ever since the Council of Ephesus in 431 declared that Mary was truly the Mother of God, it became clear that Mary was essential to understanding Jesus. The incarnation of the Son of God is forever linked to Mary.

Mozart enshrined this bond in his motet about the Holy Eucharist: *Ave Verum Corpus, ex Virgine Marie* (Hail True Body, Born of the Virgin Mary). To those who denied Christ's humanity, the Church pointed to Mary from whose bone and blood he was born.

Mary also helps us appreciate the Church more deeply. In her contemplative prayer at the Annunciation, Mary agreed to the conception of the physical body of Christ by the power of the Spirit. Thirty-three years later, Mary went to the Upper Room and led the Apostles and the 120 disciples in prayer for the coming of the Spirit. Thus, at Pentecost, Mary presided over the manifestation of the Church—the Mystical Body of Christ.

Vatican II noted Mary's intimate connection to the Church. Just as she engendered Jesus in the flesh, so the Church engenders new Christians in the baptismal font. Just as Mary is the greatest witness of faith, so is the communion of the Church an enduring people of faith. The Council went so far as to suggest a new title for her, calling her "mother of the members of Christ...since she has by her charity joined in bringing about the birth of believers in the Church, who are members of its head" ("The Church").

On November 21, 1964, during the third session of Vatican II, Paul VI, during the celebration of Mass, declared our Lady "Mother of the Church, that is, of the entire Christian people, both the faithful and their pastors, who call her their most loving mother." He decreed that "from now onward the whole Christian people should give even greater honor to the Mother of God under this most loving title" (*Acta Apostolicae Sedis*).

Spiritual Principle

Second, the Church's saints have witnessed the spiritual principle that the closer we get to Mary, the closer she brings us to Christ. In the divine plan of salvation, Mary's glorious calling was to give Jesus to the world. It was Mary who made Christ available to us. The great paintings and icons of the Madonna show her presenting Jesus to the world for salvation and adoration. Mary does not draw attention to herself, but to her Son.

Those who have had their prayers answered by Mary's intercession find themselves more intimately attracted to

Christ, especially his presence in the Eucharist. When we want a personal union with Jesus, we have a better chance of achieving this by asking Mary to be the mother who links us with him.

Saint Louis de Montfort says it plainly: "If, then, we establish solid devotion to our Blessed Lady, it is only to establish more perfectly devotion to Jesus Christ, and to provide an easy and secure means for finding Jesus Christ" (*True Devotion to Mary*).

Authentic love for Mary always generates enthusiastic love for Jesus. This love then extends to the Church, stimulates active participation in the sacraments and a commitment to works of love, justice and mercy. This is the spiritual principle that animates so many millions today.

The Principle of the Heart's Desire

The third reason for the exuberant new attention to Mary is a hunger for the supernatural. This is a desire for God planted in every human heart. At other times in history, the fulfillment of this desire was easier because the culture nurtured it. This is less true today.

Science, beneficial in so many ways, has had a dramatic influence on the last hundred years, contributing to the creation of what we call a secular culture. Science gave us the industrial revolution in the late nineteenth century and the technological revolution in the late twentieth. Rapid advances in these fields cause enormous changes that, at the very least, can be said to be distracting, obscuring the divine presence in our lives.

Because of the marvels of medicine, populations have grown enormously. People live longer and need new ways to stay on the journey of faith through many life stages. Many find it difficult to nurture and mature, with God's grace, the faith received in childhood. Just as there can be arrested development psychologically, the same is possible spiritually. Lifelong spiritual growth is just as important as other forms of development.

Due to the advance in communications, especially television, billions of images and messages unrelated to God and often hostile to religion, desensitize people to spiritual realities. It is like a war of attrition. We are daily nibbled to spiritual death by a lava flow of messages that pull us away from God.

Because modern transportation can move people at astonishing speeds, we have become a transient culture, leaving behind the villages, neighborhoods and extended families where faith was traditionally handed on. We can no longer rely upon a Christian culture to support our faith; we need consciously to rebuild what was once taken for granted.

This impact of science has been accompanied by new philosophies which rely on reason alone and are uncomfortable with faith. They support skepticism about faith as well as doubt that objective truth can ever be known.

We do not need to analyze further these causes of secular culture. This has been done by many others at greater length and with sharper insight. What is clear for us is that secularity has failed to help the hungry heart find God.

But just because there is no food does not mean the stomach ceases to growl. The soul thirsts for God even in the secular desert.

The maternal warmth of Mary is the easiest and most non-threatening road back to the spirituality we seek. In a tawdry culture, Mary is utter beauty. In the modern spiritual wasteland, Mary is a spring of fresh water. In the flattened landscape that tries to shut out all vestige of heaven, Mary is the "gate of heaven" that opens us to God.

The phenomenal "turn to Mary" in this age of unbelief is Christ's hidden weapon. It is she who tempers the harshness of a consumer culture. Just as she did at the Marriage Feast of Cana, when she said to Jesus, "They have no wine" (John 2:3), so she gazes at the watery spirituality of our times and alerts her Son again about the absence of the wine of God.

Mary rejoices in her calling to open our hearts to Jesus

and the Church. Her last words in the New Testament are, "Do whatever he tells you" (John 3:5). Her only calling is to fill us with Jesus. She points to Jesus, never to herself. When our hearts are empty she knows the secret of filling them.

Music and art often tell us best about the destiny of Mary. The poetry of the following hymn, sung to the Celtic melody, "The Flight of the Earls," connects words to the emotions—and feelings to the event of salvation to which Mary joins us.

I Sing a Maid

I sing a maid of tender years
To whom an angel came,
And knelt, as to a mighty queen,
And bowed his wings of flame:
A nation's hope in her reply,
This maid of matchless grace;
For God's own Son became her child,
And she his resting place.

She watched him grow to manhood's strength
To meet his destiny;
And when the danger of his truth
Brought him to Calvary,
She stood by him all powerless
To ease his dying pain,
'Til in the darkest hour of all,
She held her Son again.

And if the song had ended then,
Our eyes would fill with tears;
But ah! the song had just begun
To echo down the years!
Now lift your voices, hearts and souls,
To sing with one accord
To honor Mary, Mother of
The Christ, the Risen Lord.

—*M. D. Ridge*, Gather

Mary, Pray for Us

Ever since Mary intervened at Cana for the embarrassed couple faced with a wine shortage, Mary has spent her existence praying for our needs. This is what we mean when we call Mary our intercessor. Catholics know that Jesus is our only mediator with the Father, but we also believe that Mary and the saints can pray for us in Jesus and through the Spirit to the Father.

A popular story among Catholics is the case of strangers in heaven. Jesus is seen walking around the celestial city and noticing a number of people who don't belong there. Jesus goes to Peter who guards the gate and handles admissions. He asks Peter, "Do you realize there are a number of people who have no business being here? Why did you let them in?"

"It's not my fault," replied Peter. "I didn't want to say anything because I thought it would upset you." Frustrated, Jesus said, "I'm the Lord. I have a right to know what's going on." Hesitant, Peter answered, "Well the truth of the matter is that I tell them they can't get in. So they march confidently around to the back door—and your mother lets them in."

This lighthearted tale tells us how deeply Mary is embedded in the Catholic soul. For centuries, scholars have ponderously parsed the gifts of Mary and rendered countless cautions about excess. And they have a right and duty to do so. But the sons and daughters of Mary blithely go their way, knowing they have an affectionate mother who is interested in their salvation. They swell with conviction when they cry out, "Mary, pray for us!" They know she will never let them down.

While I emphasize here the Catholic vision of Mary, I should also draw your attention to other Christians who love her just as much. One outstanding example is the founder of the community of Taizé, Brother Roger, a Protestant. Taizé has become an ecumenical monastery with both Catholic and Protestant members. Since its founding, it has

been an inspiring center of spirituality, especially for young
people.

Brother Roger tells the following story about a woman
who had a vision of Mary:

> When I arrived in Taizé in 1940, I was welcomed from
> the very first days by some of the old women of the
> village who had hearts of gold. One of them, Marie
> Auboeuf, was for me like a mother according to the
> Gospel.
>
> In those days I was alone. The community did not
> exist yet. I was preparing its creation and I was offering
> shelter to people who had hidden to avoid the worst. It
> was wartime in Europe. Marie Aubeouf was poor. She
> had raised ten children. Where in her heart did she find
> the simple intuition that allowed her to understand the
> vocation I was trying to live out?
>
> That elderly woman told me that one night, many
> years before I arrived, while she was praying the rosary,
> the Virgin Mary appeared to her in a vision. The next
> morning when she got up, she was cured of a paralysis
> of the hip that was making it harder and harder for her
> to walk and to take care of her children.
>
> That appearance of the Virgin took place in Taizé
> long before I myself had even heard the name of that
> village, and yet it continues to have an effect.
>
> — *Mother Teresa of Calcutta and Brother Roger of
> Taizé*, Mary, Mother of Reconciliations

Brother Roger says he wondered how this old lady—a lifelong Catholic, probably with little education or any awareness of an ecumenical movement—could be so kind and
accepting of him and his remarkable project. Where did she
get the intuition? She simply told him the story of her vision of Mary and the healing. In some mysterious way,
Mary opened this good woman's heart to accept this new
adventure of faith that today enchants the world.

Brother Roger recalls that in his childhood, when on va-
cations, he and his sisters would often stop in at a nearby
Catholic church, usually at twilight. He remembers that

there was always a lighted candle in front of the Blessed Mother. Later, at Taizé, he kept an icon of the Virgin in the corner of his room. The candle in front of it was for him the "mirror of an inner fire."

He had received the icon from the Orthodox Patriarch Athenagoras. The illuminated icon of Mary reminded him that Christians often live in the night of faith. But then they are fed with an inner light from the Holy Spirit who burns with a fire that never goes away. That fire gives us the light of God's truth and the warmth of the Spirit's love.

Mary, a Model for Our Prayer

We not only ask Mary to pray for us, we also see her as an example for our own prayer life. After Mary's appearance at Pentecost, there is no other scriptural reference to her activity. From then on she is cloistered from the eyes of the world. She has retreated into deepest silence. Her life is now "hidden with Christ in God" (Colossians 3:3). She became the example of the praying Church.

While the apostles were engaged in active ministry converting people to Christ and establishing Christian communities, Mary supported them with her prayer. The Novgorod school of Russian icon painting created an icon of Christ's Ascension which portrays this truth of Church life. Jesus is at the top of the icon, carried by angels into glory. Mary stands on earth and in the center of the scene, still and silent, with her hands extended in prayer. Two angels clothed in white form a protective wall that separates her from the activity in the rest of the icon. Beyond the angels are the apostles—full of movement, hands waving, feet moving, bodies arched in activity—men on the move to go forth and preach the Gospel. They represent the evangelizing Church. They are the missionaries bringing Christ to the world. Mary, on the other hand, stands firmly in the center of the ecclesial community. From her rooted presence flows the prayer and stability the Church needs for fidelity to the mission of salvation. The icon portrays her as the fundamental link with Jesus. It is an ideal picture of the relationship between contemplation and action. After Pentecost that becomes Mary's gift to us.

Saints help us to appreciate the inner life of Mary as the person of prayer in the heart of the Church. Saint Thérèse of the Child Jesus is one such example. She wanted to be a missionary, a priest or a martyr. But how could she reconcile these desires with her life as a Carmelite in the small village of Lisieux? One day she solved her dilemma. She realized that if the Church is Christ's Mystical Body, that Body needed a heart. This heart gives life to the Body, otherwise it would not live.

> I knew that the Church had a heart and that such a heart appeared to be aflame with love. I knew that one love drove the members of the Church to action, that if this love were extinguished, the Apostles would have proclaimed the Church no longer....
>
> O Jesus, my love, at last I have found my calling: my call is love. Certainly I have found my proper place in the Church, and you gave me that place, my God. In the heart of the Church, my mother, I will be love...
>
> — *Liturgy of the Hours*

Mary models prayer for us in the sense that she shows us that our active lives should be supported by daily silence and meditative prayer. We need quiet time to be alone with God. Our souls need to be fed with the graces of the Spirit if we are to witness Jesus in acts of love, justice and mercy. Action without prayer soon becomes mere activism. Our deeds will cease to bear fruit for the needs of the Church and the world—and our own hearts will dry up.

The Mystery of Love

Why do we want Mary to pray for us? Why do we look to her as a model for prayer? Ultimately that we may become like Jesus who is pure love. The mystery of Mary opens us to the mystery of love. Mary was the first disciple of Jesus to become love in the heart of the Church and the world. Mary prays that this will happen to us. Mary shows us how to do it.

What is this love to which she points us? The Greeks had a word for it: *agape* (AG-a-pay). Saint John used it when he summed up everything that God means, "God is love" (1 John 4:8). God is *agape*. What does it mean?

Love is more than a feeling. Feelings come *to* us. Love comes *from* us. Feelings are like the wind which comes from all directions and sometimes does not come at all. Feelings are temperamental. We are not responsible for our feelings (though we are accountable for what we do about them). Mary could feel differently about the people she met. Like her son, she tried to love them all equally. Feelings are too unstable to pass themselves off for love.

Agape love comes from us. We are responsible for loving others. We are called to love people regardless of how we feel about them. Love means willing what is good for others. If we happen to have positive feelings—fine. But we must choose what is good for people regardless of how we feel. Love may include warm feelings, but we are called to love whether such feelings are there nor not.

Love does not deal with abstractions. I once heard someone say, "I love humanity. It's people I can't stand." That person missed the point of *agape* love, thinking of it in terms of a global abstraction. Humanity does not ring the doorbell. People do. Humanity does not beg for a handout. Homeless, hungry people do. Love only works when we realize that we are called to love individual men and women, persons who have names, histories, virtues and vices, hopes and fears just like us.

Jesus treated people as persons with names, not as numbers in a survey. The good shepherd "calls his sheep by name." Jesus establishes a personal relationship with us. "I know mine and mine know me" (John 10:3,14). Jesus did not ask us to love humanity; he said we should love our neighbor—a real knowable and lovable human being. Mary, too, loved in a concrete and singular manner, such as when she went to her cousin Elizabeth to help her with the birth of her forthcoming baby.

Love is more than kindness. Agape love includes kindness, but it is greater than what is considered the kindly thing to do. Generally, we think of kindness as compassion or the relief of suffering. Normally we are expected to be kind to strangers, but we do a little more than that when dealing with our relatives and friends. We are kind to pets, but we sometimes have to be tough with those we love. Tough love has a place in Christian behavior.

It has been said that grandfathers are kind, but fathers are demanding. The world has room for gentler behavior, but love often requires a sharp rebuke and a flash of anger. Jesus was not sentimental with Peter when the apostle wanted to keep him from the Cross. Jesus barked at Peter, "Get behind me, Satan! You are an obstacle to me. You are not thinking as God does, but as human beings do" (Matthew 16:23). Mary was not afraid to be confrontational with her twelve-year-old when he stayed at the Temple without her permission. Her love did not prevent her from mentioning the anxiety he caused her and Joseph. True love is honest and not always sweet and "feel-good." It is often demanding.

Love wills the good and gives the self. Essentially, love is an act of the will, a choice on behalf of the good of others. In everyday life it involves giving oneself away—within moral limits, of course. We can find out who we really are by giving ourselves to others. Saint Francis expressed it: "It is in giving that I receive." The Son of God loved us by giving away the status of divine glory so that he might become human like us in all things, save sin. Jesus spent his life giving himself away.

In his passion, it would have been understandable if he indulged in a little self-pity or self-protectiveness, but he didn't. He continued to use whatever energies he had left to heal the ear of Malchus, glance with forgiveness at the Peter who denied him, assure the repentant thief he would be saved, pray to the Father for forgiveness of his persecutors and entrust his mother to John and the Church to his mother.

Agape creates love where it did not exist. *Agape* fills the lover with more love each time it is given away. Even if the love we give to another is refused, we have more love than before. That's why we can never tire of loving, since we will have so much more to give, finding our only joy in giving it. Once possessed by *agape*, we cannot *not* love.

Conclusion

I believe we are witnessing today a "turn" to Mary of amazing magnitude. All generations continue to bless Mary even in this most secular of cultures. The theological principle behind it is the truth that understanding Mary is necessary for appreciating the meaning and mission of Jesus and the Church.

The spiritual principle driving the Marian revival is the truth that the closer we get to Mary the nearer we come to Jesus and the Church. Mary connects us intimately with Christ and brings us home to Mother Church, the sacraments and the ecclesial witness of love, justice and mercy in the world.

The hunger-of-the-heart principle teaches us that there is a warm welcome back to God through the maternal affection of Mary. She helps us bypass the hypnosis of the secular culture. We recognize again the inborn drive of our hearts to God and return to Christ and the Church.

urpose of it all is to experience ever more effec-
ist's salvation from sin and his gift of divine life.
....ne life moves us to prayer which should result in
agape love, the love God is.

This is why so many millions love Mary. This is why
you and I love her, too.

Reflection

Let's consider more deeply the three reasons for the special
attraction Mary holds for the faithful and plant them firmly
in our hearts.

Theological Principle. From the earliest days of the Church,
the saints realized that knowing Mary would help us know
Christ and the Church. The first heresy that faced the
Church came from the Gnostics. They found it hard to accept that Jesus was really human. They denied that he had
flesh and bones that could be born of a woman. They rejected the belief that he had a body which could die on a
Cross. They repudiated the faith that he even retained his
body in a glorified form after his Resurrection.

The faith of the Church began to focus on the Virgin
Mary as Christ's real mother, truly begetting him in the
flesh by the power of the Spirit. The birth of Jesus stories in
Matthew and Luke made it clear that Jesus was born of the
Virgin Mary. As objections to his humanity grew, the
Church understood more clearly why Mary's role was es-
sential in defending this truth about Jesus. That was a seed
of faith that linked Mary to Jesus in many new and fruitful
ways throughout Church history to this very day. With our
faith seeking understanding, we appreciate better how
Mary opens the door to understanding Christ and his
Church.

✱ *How much have I grown in understanding Mary throughout
my life?*

✳ *How has Mary helped me understand Jesus?*

✳ *What does Mary teach me about the meaning of the Church?*

Spiritual Principle. There is a popular Catholic saying: "To Jesus through Mary with a smile." As an axiom of piety it illustrates the spiritual teaching that proximity to Mary draws us closer to Jesus. When the fathers of Vatican II debated where to put their teaching about Mary, they decided to place it in the constitution on the Church. So, Mary not only creates in us an intimacy with Jesus, but also a relationship with the Church.

Mary called herself the handmaid of the Lord. She could also say she is the handmaid of the Church. When the sculptors added their masterpieces to the doors and walls of medieval cathedrals, they shaped Mary as a crowned queen mother, with her outstretched arms holding Jesus front and center for our attention. By putting her over the main doors of these Gothic houses of worship, the sculptors implicitly made her the official welcomer to Christ's Church. Mary has no interest in her own glory. She is happiest when Jesus is praised and loved. She enjoys fresh peace when we are reconciled to the Church and the sacraments and Christian witness. She is the star of evangelization.

✳ *In what ways have I come to a deeper love for Jesus because of my affection for Mary?*

✳ *How does Mary intensify my active membership in the Church and active participation in the sacraments and Christian witness?*

✳ *Cite examples from others' lives which show the power of Mary in bringing them to Jesus and the Church.*

Hunger-of-the-Heart Principle. It seems as though the more secular our culture becomes the more fervent is the "turn" to Mary. The heart wants God no matter what the culture tells us. Mary figures prominently in this situation because she is the most accessible spiritual presence in a culture wildly running away from God, yet investing in any number of cults, superstitions and fortune-tellings.

Mary is an authentic gateway to heaven amid all the false ones. Lost souls feel at home with her because they believe she knows what an empty heart feels like. They trust her to bring them God and are not deceived or betrayed by the Holy Mother. In New Testament times, the city of Ephesus boasted of one of the seven wonders of the world, the temple of the goddess Artemis—a mere useless statue.

All that is left of that temple is one standing column. Artemis is gone, but Mary is still around. Even at Ephesus today, where all else is classical ruins, there is a House of Mary, said by some to have been her home with Saint John. To this house pilgrims come from all over the world. Mary touches hearts in a secular time, not for her own benefit, but in order to bring us to Christ and the Church.

✳ *What are some stories you could tell of people you know who have "bought into" secular culture, yet experience a hunger of the heart which this culture does not satisfy?*

✳ *How could you help such people get in touch with Mary?*

✳ *When you are alone and in a thoughtful mood, how do you experience the hunger for God?*

Prayer

Father, may the prayers of the Virgin Mary bring us closer to Christ and the Church. Through her intercession may we participate in the sacraments more actively and dedicate ourselves to a Christian witness of love, justice and mercy. Help us to see how you intended Mary to be part of your divine plan of salvation. We ask this through your Son in the Spirit. Amen.

Henry Ossawa Tanner
ANNUNCIATION
1898
Philadelphia Museum of Art
The W. P. Wilstach Collection

CHAPTER TWO

※

Woman of Faith

Who would know how to proclaim your grandeur?

You have embellished human nature,

You have surpassed angelic legions,

You have surpassed all creatures...

We acclaim you: Hail full of grace!

—*Sophronius of Jerusalem*

I Prayed to Mary for Help

I also developed a devotion to Mary during my time in
the (New Age) community that made it easier for me to
come into the Catholic Church. Shortly after I joined the
community, the man with whom I had been about to
have an affair came to supper. Afterward he leaned a
little toward me and began to put out a sexual energy
that almost pulled me under. I prayed to Mary for help
and immediately felt uplifted and freed. This happened
three times and then he left. I continued to go to Mary
in prayer, seeking her help in becoming more gentle
and pure of heart. Another community woman and I
went to a workshop on feminine spirituality organized
by some new age groups and I did a presentation on
Mary....

The emotional resistance to the Church I had felt
for so long had melted away, and I was at peace. I was
received on June 24, 1980.

—*Celia Wolf-Devine*, "From New Age Christianity
to the Catholic Church"

In her faith testimony about her conversion, Celia Wolf-
Devine shares with us the role of Mary who accompanied
her on her journey into the Church. The woman of faith
walked with Celia to the faith. Mary has walked with me as
well through the stages of my life. I recall my days as a sem-
inarian at Saint Norbert College, De Pere, Wisconsin, in the
late forties. Each summer, over three hundred sisters came
there to complete their bachelor's degrees.

Clothed in their many different habits, they brought
color and pageantry to the campus. They also supplied outstanding professors for the summer courses. I shall always
remember Sister Chrysostom of the School Sisters of Notre
Dame, from Milwaukee's Mount Mary College. Her lec-
tures on Chaucer and Browning were events of wisdom. It
was a time when the classics and the liberal arts needed little defense: Shakespeare was in his heaven and all was
right with the world.

Besides the liturgies at Saint Joseph's College Church, the principal spiritual event of the summer was the Living Rosary. One night just before the last week of school, when the dark had settled in, the sisters created a candlelight procession beginning among the old oak trees north of Main Hall. They produced a rosary of light, accompanied by the prayers and mysteries and a sequence of traditional hymns. Their talented *schola cantorum* sang harmonies to honor Mary, the woman of faith.

These sisters were hard-working women who staffed Catholic elementary schools in parishes around the Great Lakes. They passed on the Catholic faith to thousands of children. They knew they were brides of Christ—and also affirmed they were sisters of his Mother Mary. Like a pilgrim people, they paraded across our campus, singing and praying as they went until they came to the statue of Mary which is in front of Burke Hall. They formed a human rosary around the image of Mary.

The evening always ended with the "Salve Regina" ("Hail, Holy Queen") sung in Latin to a Gregorian chant melody. I sensed a mystical quality about these annual services. The warm Wisconsin night, the starlight, the temperate but affecting religious fervor focused us on Mary, yet somehow she turned us immediately to Christ. It seems incongruous to call it a night of faith, since in fact it led us to light.

Seven Traits of Faith

In this chapter we will consider the faith of Mary as it is presented in the New Testament. There are many ways to consider this testimony and all of them help us appreciate her. I have adapted these seven traits of faith from the *Catechism of the Catholic Church*, and connected them to her story in Scripture.

Mary's faith is personal. Faith begins only after God approaches us. In Scripture we call this God's revelation of himself. God speaks; the listener is invited to respond. Hence the first act of faith is a personal response to God: *I believe*. The call is Trinitarian. We hear a call from the Father, made personal in Jesus and experienced through the power of the Spirit. The Spirit gives us the capacity to respond with a "Yes, Lord." This "yes" is an act of obedience to God's call from our mind, will, heart and soul.

At the annunciation, Mary is called to make an act of personal faith. She is a young virgin, betrothed to Joseph. God sends the angel Gabriel to Mary, asking her consent to be part of the divine plan of salvation. The angel does not call her by name, but addresses her as a "highly favored one," a woman "full of grace."

Normally, heavenly visions frighten people, so the messengers say, "Do not be afraid." But Gabriel troubles Mary not by his appearance, but by his words. He doesn't frighten Mary, but he does puzzle her. Why would God say she is full of grace and favor? Gabriel explains that God wants her to conceive a son and name him Jesus. This child will be called the Son of the Most High, he will mount the throne of David and rule an eternal kingdom.

This message confuses her all the more. Mary knows from Scripture that God will send a messiah. But this angel reveals that God wants *her* to be the mother of the messiah. Is this possible? She needs the deepest faith to make a proper reply.

When faced with a similar announcement, Zechariah had questioned Gabriel. He doubted that a woman of his wife's advanced age could conceive. Mary has a different problem. She is a virgin, pledged to marry Joseph. According to tradition, they have planned to live together in mutual virginity.

When Mary questions Gabriel, though, it is not from doubt but from a fullness of faith. She seeks to understand God's meaning, to know *how* this will be possible. Gabriel tells her that the conception will be caused by the Holy Spirit. He adds that Mary's cousin Elizabeth has already been blessed with an unlikely pregnancy.

Mary's positive response is an "obedience of faith," an expression used by Saint Paul (Romans 16:26). The word *obedience* comes from a Latin word meaning "to hear." In this context, God speaks and Mary hears with her heart. She gives God the obedience of faith.

Mary understands that her reply must arise from the deepest part of her faith life. She responds with a personal act of faith: "May it be done to me according to your word" (Luke 1:38). At creation, God said, "Let it be done." In this new creation, Mary sings, "May it be done." She has received a revelation. She has obeyed with faith.

We may compare Mary to Abraham. He is our father in faith who sired the people of God, the people of Israel. Mary is our mother in faith who gives birth to the savior, who brings all people to God. Never has faith been more personal or creative.

Mary's faith is a grace. Gabriel tells Mary she is "full of grace." Later, we will apply this truth to her Immaculate Conception. Here, we will consider the link between grace and faith. Some people have such strong intellects they think they can reason themselves into faith. Others imagine they can convert people to Christ by well thought-out arguments. But faith is a gift from God, not the result of clever thinking.

When the brilliant Clare Booth Luce, devastated by the death of her daughter, went to see Father Fulton Sheen, she was prepared for a battle of wits. There was such a battle, but the only victory came one day as she talked about her lost child, shedding a flood of tears while Sheen listened quietly. She recalls that they were soon kneeling before the shrine of Mary in his chapel; the gift of faith had overtaken her heart.

Some speak of the "leap" of faith. They realize that reason cannot produce faith. Rather, having exhausted all arguments and protests, the seeker leaps across the chasm of doubt and unbelief to the haven of faith. But this is just another version of self-produced faith. Faith is not a leap; it's a gift. We don't jump across a chasm. The Spirit carries us across, into the arms of God. The following verse from a popular song says it well:

> Did I ever tell you, you're my hero,
> And everything I want to be?
> I can soar higher than an eagle.
> You are the wind beneath my wings.
>   —*Larry Henley*, "Wind Beneath My Wings"

Grace is the wind beneath the wings of our faith.

One of America's best-known intellectuals is Mortimer Adler, a Jewish philosopher and guru of the Great Books program. In his early career he was admired by Catholics for his mastery of the works of Thomas Aquinas. Many wondered why he did not become a Catholic. How could he explain Aquinas so persuasively and yet remain outside the Church?

His standard answer was, "I am not a Catholic precisely because I understand a teaching of Aquinas so well. Faith is a gift and I have not received this grace."

Thomas Merton's poem, "The Quickening of John the Baptist," retells the story of Mary's visit to her cousin Elizabeth. Merton sees Mary leaving behind the lemon trees, the yellow fishing boats, the oil presses and the wine-smelling yards. Her clothes fly like sails. What truth lies behind her eyes, grey as doves?

The moment Mary greets her cousin, the child in Elizabeth's womb leaps. Merton likens Mary's salutation to the sound of a monastery bell which calls us to faith. Merton wonders about Mary's voice. What secret syllable did she pronounce that awakened the unborn John to a "dance of faith?"

Merton expected no words, no verbal explanation of a divine mystery. John's body talk said it all. It is a time to let grace have its way. Teachings and explanations will come in due time.

Elizabeth praises Mary, "Blessed are you who believed"

(Luke 1:45). Mary had given God an undivided heart. The surrender of her person and the hospitality of her body for the divine child illustrated the grace of her faith more than any words. Reason and faith are friends, but have different origins—a human source for reason and a divine grace for faith.

The grace of faith made Mary the new Eve. Eve (and Adam) had received the graces of faith which would have kept them obedient to God's will. Where Eve failed, Mary succeeded. Mary allowed the grace of faith to help her hear and obey the Word of the Lord.

During her visit to Elizabeth, Mary praised God with her Magnificat. Mary's song is a pure tribute to the power of grace that enabled her to believe. The Church sings it every evening during the Liturgy of the Hours in thousands of rectories, monasteries, convents and Christian homes. Mary attributes everything she has to God. For her, all is grace.

Mary's faith is free. Faith is like love. Love cannot be forced or imposed. The same is true of faith, which by its nature is a free, human response. Jesus invited people to faith and conversion but never coerced them. Jesus bore witness to the truth, but refused to impose it on anyone. He could have summoned legions of angels to defend him, but he did not. Jesus used no spectacular forms of logic or manipulation to convince anyone to believe. He simply offered the witness of his life.

This is not to say that Jesus was indifferent to scriptural teaching and God's moral law. When the rich young man asked what he should do to have eternal life, Jesus told him to keep the commandments. Jesus was faithful to the Mosaic covenant and invited others to be as well. Jesus roared like a prophet when he cleansed the temple. He wanted people to be free to choose, but also to be responsible for the choices they made.

Pope John Paul II considers himself an evangelizer; this is especially evident in his dozens of visits to the nations of the world. But he calls his method a "dialogue of salvation." He shares his faith with those who believe and those who do not. Like Christ, the Pope is not indifferent about the Church's moral teachings—he, too, has often thundered like a prophet. He insists that responsibility is the proper way to exercise freedom. In his meetings with young people, John Paul likes to invite them to belief, "I offer you the option for Christ. I present to you the option for love." There is an affectionate urgency in his appeal, but there is no suggestion of force. He honors their freedom. He proposes Christ; he does not impose the Lord upon them.

Mary exercises her faith freely. Gabriel does not threaten her at the annunciation. He asks her; he does not order her. At the same time the angel knows that Mary is a responsible woman. She is aware of her moral and religious duties and these must accompany any use of her freedom.

Saint Bernard has a wonderful homily on the annunciation that perfectly illustrates this point. The Church uses his homily on December 20 for the Office of Readings. Bernard sets the scene dramatically: Gabriel has spoken and awaits a reply. The silence that follows contains the tension of a turning point in history. Biblical figures line up like a chorus in a Greek play to beg, urge, plead and pester Mary to hurry up and say yes. The scene has the quality of a medieval mystery play.

> Tearful Adam begs it. Abraham begs it. David begs it.
> All the other holy patriarchs, your ancestors, ask it of
> you... Answer quickly, O Virgin. Reply in haste to the
> angel, or rather through the angel to the Lord. Answer
> with a word, receive the Word of God. Speak your own
> word, conceive the divine Word. Breathe a passing
> word, embrace the eternal Word....Though modest
> silence is pleasing, dutiful speech is now more
> necessary. Open your heart to faith, O Blessed Virgin.
> —*Liturgy of the Hours*

Bernard puts the pressure on Mary indeed, but it is a holy anxiety for the accomplishment of salvation. It is quite clear he believes Mary is free. His plea is urgent, but his respect for her freedom is profound.

We should be ready to follow the example of Mary who freely and responsibly showed a readiness to do God's will. She accepted the angel's message and welcomed the eternal Son. The Spirit filled her with light and she became the Temple of the Word.

Mary's faith is full of conviction. The eleventh chapter of *Hebrews* contains one of the best passages on faith in the entire Bible. The opening verse describes faith as conviction and assurance: "Now faith is the assurance of things hoped for, the conviction of things not seen" (NRSV). Then in verse after verse the author cites the heroes and heroines of faith in Scripture.

One of the oddest facets of our scientific age is the widespread feeling of insecurity. Science is designed to give us confidence and assurance with visible, concrete proofs. After all, seeing is believing. All around us is tangible evidence of what science and technology can do for us. We are trained from childhood to say, "Show me," and expect to be satisfied. But the constant flow of contradictory studies and the shortcomings of science can confuse rather than reassure.

Just as odd is the fact that people with religious faith are frequently rocks of assurance and conviction. Yet believers deal with what is "not seen" and with what is "hoped for." The eternal realities of heaven, angels, the Trinity, grace, resurrection, salvation from sin and everlasting life cannot be seen in the same way one can examine the life of a cell under a microscope or the marvels of space. Like the Eucharist, they are mysteries of faith. For people of faith, "Believing is seeing."

We can see the results of faith in the heroic lives of the saints and in inspiring acts of concern for the hungry, the ill and the oppressed. The world's most convinced people have their faith in the unseen. The most assured people have graced faith in a hope that has yet to be fulfilled. Their observable witness as persons of admirable moral character and spiritual depth is incontestable. Yet the source of their conviction and assurance remains invisible.

Even when the Son of God actually became visible in Jesus, it still took faith to "see" him. At the Last Supper, Philip said to Jesus, "Lord, show us the Father, and we will be satisfied." Jesus replied, "Have I been with you all this time, Philip, and you still do not know me? Whoever has seen me has seen the Father" (John 14:8-9).

Philip had seen Jesus, marveled at his miracles, listened to his magnificent sermons, taken long hikes with the Master, shared in hundreds of debates and dinner conversations, felt the personal magnetism of Christ and still did not know who Jesus really was. Even when he saw the risen Jesus, he thought it was a ghost. The Gospels show how much Christ himself struggled to help the apostles to come to faith. And he would need to send the Holy Spirit to abide with them to sustain and nourish their faith.

But once the apostles had faith they were transformed into rocks of conviction. All of them displayed an astonishing courage and selfless energy in witnessing Christ. They not only had faith, they kept it and developed it.

The faith of Mary is a similar example of assurance and conviction. The Gospels have several accounts of a scene that seems to divert attention from Mary and even diminish her role. "While he was speaking, a woman from the crowd called out and said to him, 'Blessed is the womb that carried you and the breasts which you nursed.' He replied, 'Rather, blessed are those who hear the word of God and observe it'" (Luke 11:27-28).

A variation of this occasion describes Mary and the family standing at the edge of the crowd and wanting to meet with him. In Matthew 12:49-50, Jesus stretches his hands to the disciples and says, "Here are my mother and my brothers, for whoever does the will of my heavenly Father is my brother, sister and mother." Mark 3:34 pictures Jesus as "looking around at those seated in the circle" and calling them his relatives, again repeating the words about doing the will of God. Pope John Paul II addresses the obvious question:

> Is Jesus thereby distancing himself from his mother according to the flesh? Does he perhaps wish to leave her in the hidden obscurity which she herself has chosen? If this seems to be the case from the tone of these words, one must nevertheless note that the new and different motherhood which Jesus speaks of to his disciples refers precisely to Mary in a very special way. Is not Mary the first of those who hear the word of God and do it? And therefore, does not the blessing uttered by Jesus in response to the woman in the crowd refer primarily to her? ...We can say the blessing proclaimed by Jesus is not in opposition, despite appearances, to the blessing uttered by the unknown woman, but rather coincides with the blessing in the person of this Virgin Mother, who called herself only "the handmaid of the Lord" (Luke 1:38).
> —*The Mother of the Redeemer*

The conviction and assurance of faith only occur in those who stay on the journey. The first fervor of faith is not enough. We are expected to remain faithful to the will of God throughout all our life stages with all their challenges. Mary did this from the moment she said yes at the annunciation to the day she slept in the Lord and was assumed into heaven. This made her a convinced and assured believer.

Mary's faith is nourished by the message of salvation. Up to this point I have placed before you these traits of Mary's faith: Her faith is personal, free, graced and full of conviction. These are all comments about the relational aspect of her faith. They tell us how she relates to God.

Now I must take up another side of her faith, namely, her unshakable belief in the message of salvation. Jesus said, "I am the truth" (John 14:6). By that he meant that he personalized the truth, witnessed it. Because he was the

Son of God, he was truth itself.

But Jesus also taught truth as a message. His Sermon on the Mount, parables and wisdom sayings are examples of the truths he taught. All of his teachings explained the divine plan of salvation from sin and the consequent gift of divine life. He had a message.

We live in a time that favors the personal. Pope Paul VI understood this when he said that modern people listen more willingly to witnesses than to teachers. If they pay attention to teachers, it is because they are witnesses.

But Pope Paul also emphasized the necessity of preaching the message of salvation. He quoted Saint Paul in this regard:

> But are they to call on one in whom they have not believed? And how are they to believe in one of whom they have never heard? And how are they to hear without someone to proclaim him? ...So faith comes from what is heard, and what is heard comes through the word of Christ.
> —*Romans 10:14,17*

Pope Paul adds these comments:

> The fatigue produced these days by so much empty talk and the relevance of many other forms of communication must not however diminish the permanent power of the word, or cause a loss of confidence in it. The word remains ever relevant, especially when it is the bearer of the power of God. This is why Saint Paul's axiom, "Faith comes from what is heard" (Romans 10:17), also retains its relevance: It is the word that is heard which leads to belief.
> —*On Evangelization*

Mary's faith was nourished by the message of salvation found in the Hebrew Scriptures and in the teachings she experienced in her lifetime, those that accompanied the birth of Jesus and those of Jesus himself.

We have already noted the message Mary heard from the angel Gabriel. She believed the word and conceived the Word. We can infer her appreciation of the Hebrew Scriptures from her Magnificat which weaves a number of scriptural texts into a new canticle of praise.

When the shepherds come to adore Jesus they arrive with the message of the angel, "I am bringing to you good news of great joy for all the people: to you is born this day in the city of David a savior, who is the Messiah and the Lord" (Luke 2:10-11).

Then come the Magi who have followed a star, and a prophecy from Micah (5:1) that led them to Jesus. Mary hears their story, watches them adore her son and accepts the gifts of gold, frankincense and myrrh.

Mary retains these messages about her son, "reflecting on them in her heart" (Luke 2:19).

When Mary and Joseph present Jesus in the Temple, they are approached by an old man and an old woman. Simeon takes the baby in his arms. Mary hears Simeon compose the first human hymn created out of love for her son. Simeon tells her that her son will be the occasion of the fall and rise of many and that a sword will pierce her own soul. His somber prediction casts a shadow over an otherwise happy event.

At that moment the widow and prophetess Anna comes to cheer them up. With a great smile on her face and arms outspread she embraces them and praises God for their child. Twelve years later Mary and Joseph come to the Temple again to find their lost son. Jesus says, "Did you not know I must be in my father's house?" (Luke 2:49).

Once again Mary's faith holds on to these messages from Simeon, Anna and her son. "His mother treasured all these things in her heart" (Luke 2:51). They are part of her contact with the mystery of God.

> And this is how Mary for many years lives in intimacy
> with the mystery of her son and continues in her
> "pilgrimage of faith"... The first human creature thus

permitted to discover Christ was Mary, who lived with
Joseph in the same house at Nazareth.... Jesus was
aware that "no one knows the Son except the Father,"
(cf. Matthew 11:27); thus even his Mother, to whom had
been revealed most completely the mystery of divine
sonship, lived in intimacy with this mystery only
through faith!
    —*Pope John Paul II*, The Mother of the Redeemer

Mary's faith includes the cross. "When Jesus saw his
mother and the disciple there whom he loved, he said to his
mother, 'Woman, here is your son.' Then he said to the disciple, 'Here is your mother'" (John 19:26-27a).

The setting for these words at the cross is like the reading of a will. In an oral culture, the last testament is spoken
in front of family witnesses. Jesus asks John to take care of
his mother. "And from that hour the disciple took her into
his house" (John 19:27b).

Jesus also gives a commission to his mother. He addresses her as "woman" instead of "mother," as he did at
Cana. Catholic commentators note that if he had called her
mother, he would only be referring to her physical parent-
age. By speaking to her as woman, he elevated her to a maternal role in the history of salvation. He spoke to her
motherhood in the spirit, appointing her to be solicitous for
the needs of people, especially their need for salvation.

At Cana the simple story of a wine shortage at a village
wedding assumed a theological significance. Mary intercedes for the couple, telling Jesus about the wine problem.
Jesus responds, "Woman, what concern is that to you and
to me? My hour has not yet come."

His use of the term *woman* in this context guides our
minds back to Genesis 2:23 and the creation of Eve who is
called *the woman*. Jesus seems to say that Mary is the new
woman participating in the beginning of the new creation.
Moreover, Jesus says his "hour" had not come. In John's
Gospel the use of the word "hour" referred to the time
when Christ's redemptive mission would publicly begin.

Mary's faith prompts her to press him to begin his salvation mission at that moment. Jesus responds to her at that level, seeming to resist embarking on the road to the cross. Mary persists, using the words that inaugurate her role as our intercessor, her last words in the Bible: "Do whatever he tells you" (John 2:5b).

In the Gospel, Jesus hears her prayer and changes the water into wine. But he creates more than relief and joy at a wedding; he manifests his glory—his divine presence engaged in saving us from sin and offering us divine life. Thus, the salvation story begins in earnest.

Now at the cross, Mary hears her theological title "woman" again and her commission to be the spiritual mother of believers. Her faith receives this call in the most tragic of circumstances. Simeon was right. A sword does pierce her heart. She stands by her son, all helpless to ease his dying pain. She accepts her vocation to be a spiritual mother just when she is losing her physical son. Of all those who were plunged into the night and suffering of faith, Mary endures the worst—and yet remains faithful.

Her faith holds on to the belief that the salvation process had begun at Cana and had reached an extraordinary fulfillment at the cross. The two settings—Cana and Calvary—are like an altarpiece, twin works that have a unified message. Cana invites us to turn to Mary as our intercessor. Calvary moves us to invoke her as our mother.

There is a well-known passage of Origen on the presence of Mary and John on Calvary. When he speaks of John as the first Gospel, he means the deepest Gospel:

> The Gospels are the firstfruits of all Scripture and the Gospel of John is the first of the Gospels: no one can grasp its meaning without having leaned his head on Jesus' breast and having received from Jesus Mary as Mother.
> —*Commentary on John*

Mary's faith is ecclesial and communal. At the beginning
of this chapter, we saw how Mary's faith is personal. She
surrendered her whole person with an "I believe." At the
annunciation she is alone with God's messenger. In the
final appearance of Mary in Scripture, she is in the middle
of the community of believers. We see her in the upper
room leading the apostles and the 120 disciples in prayer
for the coming of the Spirit.

She is there when the Holy Spirit descends upon them
all and manifests the Church. Mary's faith and their faith is
more than a personal "I believe." It is also now a communal, ecclesial "We believe."

Faith is not an isolated act. No one can believe alone
just as no one can live without help from others. God has
given us our faith through others—our family, teachers,
friends, priests, sisters. We are expected to share our faith
with others. The gift we received needs to be handed on to
others.

In the Apostles' Creed we begin with "I believe," thus
expressing the Church's faith personally, especially at baptism. Each Sunday in the Nicene Creed we start with "We
believe," affirming that we share in the faith of the one,
holy, Catholic and apostolic Church.

At Pentecost the Church begins its pilgrimage of faith.
Mary has already begun hers at the annunciation. She has
gone before the Church in her faith journey. "As Saint
Ambrose taught, the Mother of God is a type of the Church
in the order of faith, charity and perfect union with Christ"
("The Church"). At Pentecost she is not apart from the
Church but in its very midst in communion with the members. Her faith is communal as well as personal. She holds
a special place among them for she is like a mirror in which
is reflected the wonders of God.

That community of believers knew Jesus. They knew he
was the son of Mary, that she was a unique and privileged
witness to the mystery of the Incarnation. In the upper
room, the Church looked at Mary through the window of
Jesus. Today, the Church looks at Jesus through the translu-

cent witness of Mary.

Here is the first human to believe in Jesus. Mary followed Christ step by step on her pilgrimage of faith. Mary's faith never failed. At Calvary she was like Abraham who "believed, hoping against hope" (Romans 4:18). At Pentecost her faith is fulfilled as she stands with the disciples as the first exceptional witness to Christ. Fervent in prayer, the Church contemplated her in the light of the Word made flesh.

Mary belongs absolutely to the Church. She is in communion with us. Just as truly the Church is in absolute communion with Mary. We belong with her. This is the profound meaning behind our belief that Mary's faith is communal. God's plan to save us placed Mary as mother of Jesus at Bethlehem and mother of the Church at Pentecost.

Conclusion

We have considered the story of Mary as it reflects seven characteristics of her faith: personal, graced, free, convinced, focused on a message, involved in the cross and communal.

These various expressions of faith emerged gradually as Mary proceeded on her pilgrimage of faith. It should comfort and inspire us to know that Mary realizes what we face as we embark on our own faith journey. In communion with us she walks with us and the whole Church. Like those at Pentecost we can see her through Jesus—and Jesus through her.

We should let no day pass without getting closer to Mary. She knows our needs and her maternal heart wants to love and care for us. This will not distract us from Christ or the Church or our response to the mercy, justice and salvation that others need. Like the moon that points gratefully to the sun for its light, Mary's purpose is to point us to Jesus and the Church and the needs of others. Saint Bernard liked to think of her as a star in the night guiding those on the pilgrimage of faith. So he taught, "Look at a star. Call on Mary."

Good advice, don't you think?

Reflection

This section on Mary as a woman of faith shows how rich a gift faith is. Sometimes, faith is thought of as only belief in a message, or simply a relationship with Christ. By considering the example of Mary, we come to understand that faith includes these things, but means much more.

As a reflection, consider the seven traits of faith exemplified by Mary. Look at each characteristic below and write out one sentence about your own faith that you would like to see improve. Then ask Mary for God's help in developing that aspect of your faith.

Seven Traits of Faith

* My faith is personal.

_____

_____

* My faith is free.

_____

_____

* My faith is a work of grace.

_____

_____

* My faith is full of conviction and assurance.

_____

_____

✳ My faith includes belief in the message of Christ and
the Church.

_____

_____

✳ My faith brings me to the cross.

_____

_____

✳ My faith is ecclesial and communal.

_____

_____

Prayer

Dear Father, I ask the intercession of Mary. I ask her prayers
to help me deepen my faith and advance on the pilgrimage
of faith as she did. I need help with each of these seven
traits of faith. I believe this will bring me closer to Christ
and the Church and the many needs of the people I love
and serve. I ask this of you through Jesus in the Spirit.
Amen.

Michael O'Neill McGrath, O.S.F.S.
QUEEN OF HEAVEN, MOTHER OF EARTH
1998
Collection of the artist

CHAPTER THREE

***

The New Eve

*T*he knot of Eve's disobedience

was untied by Mary's obedience.

What the virgin Eve bound by her disbelief,

Mary loosened by her faith.

—*Saint Irenaeus*

Mary Has Been Real for Me

I see all these women that I know, all these men I know,
who have enormous devotion to Mary and who have
very normal, very ordinary, very complicated lives
rooted in a faith that gives them strength. It [this
devotion] helps them to be good people, to deal with
the suffering that they have and that has an enormous
strength-giving aspect even at the same time it has some
less appealing dimensions.

Mary...has been real for me so long that, in some
ways, that precedes the scholarly dimensions. But what
I refuse to do is to assume that they are incompatible.
That's the crucial thing: that I won't give up Mary and I
won't give up the faith that scholarly study [of feminist
works] will give us more insight into the questions.
    —*Dr. Una Cadegan*, "Feminism and Mary,"
        St. Anthony Messenger

Dr. Una Cadegan is an assistant professor of history at the
University of Dayton. She says she has always taken Mary
seriously. One of thirty-five grandchildren, she was singled
out for attention by her Irish grandmother. Cadegan does
not know why, but she received a rosary from this grandmother every time a visiting relative returned from Ireland.

She says that devotion to Mary "is part of the fabric of
everything as far back as I can remember." She always
keeps a rosary in her purse. Her mother pinned a miraculous medal baby pin to her diaper—a pin Cadegan counts
among her childhood treasures. As a scholar and woman of
faith, she probes modern feminism looking for what is useful and criticizing what is not.

I can identify with Una Cadegan's remark that Mary
has always been part of the fabric of her life. In so many
ways that happened to me. When I was in fourth grade,
Sister Maria gave me a holy card with the image of Our
Lady of Guadalupe on it. Compared to the familiar images
in St. Patrick's Church, this was a strange portrayal of Mary
for me.

It did not occur to me to wonder why sister gave me such an odd picture of Mary. Only in high school did I get her point. I discovered that my birthday, which is December 12, happens to be the feast of Our Lady of Guadalupe. One day a buddy of mine, Bob Moccia, and I were talking about our mutual astrological sign, Sagittarius, which supposedly makes us optimistic persons.

It was then I realized I was born under a better sign. I said to Bob, "But I'm really a Guadalupe." Many years later I had the good fortune to be on mission for four years in Albuquerque, New Mexico, where the devotion to the Virgin of Guadalupe is alive and joyful. I have also been on pilgrimage twice to her shrine in Mexico City. The Mexicans fondly call her *la Morenita* (the little darkling). She has been a powerful and protective presence for me.

Already, we have reflected on the mystery of Mary and her calling as a woman of faith. Now we will consider the way the early Church thought of Mary. Christians began writing about her from as early as A.D. 150. We will begin with a summary of the first book written on Mary and follow this with the theme of Mary as the new Eve, considering why this image was so important in Church teaching.

The Book of James

We must understand right away that we are not discussing the *Letter of James* in the New Testament. That is sacred Scripture. This book belongs to a collection of writings known as *apocrypha*. In determining which books were truly sacred Scripture, the Church used the term *canonical* to refer to authentic scriptural texts. The apocryphal texts were those that seemed like scriptural writings but were judged by the Church to be fanciful, legendary or lacking in facts and therefore non-canonical works.

Today, some would classify apocrypha as devotional works. Others might associate them with private revelations. How did these texts come to be? To a great extent they were creations of popular imagination. Many were curious about the people named in the New Testament—they wanted details. Apocryphal writings filled in those details.

Writers continue to do the same today. Norman Mailer's novel, *The Gospel of the Son*, is an imaginary autobiography of Jesus. *The Last Temptation of Christ*, by Nikos Kazantzakis, and *The Robe*, by Lloyd Douglas, are other popular examples of this genre. These biblical novels are often just as fanciful as their apocryphal ancestors.

The original title of the *Book of James* (sometimes called the *Protoevangelium*) was the *Nativity of Mary*. It is in the final paragraph that the author gives his identity: "Now I, James, wrote this history." There is no evidence that this author, James, is one of the Apostles. Even in the Eastern Church (where his work has been better known), the Church Fathers speak of him only as "a certain James." The Western Church long rejected the influence of the book and for some centuries even condemned it.

Once you read the following retelling of the story, you will realize why it became so influential in Marian studies. Rather than give you a third-person narrative, I will use Joachim as a first-person narrator.

Joachim's Story

God made me a rich man. Praise God. I am nearing the end of my life and in my will I have pledged large sums for the poor and a major gift to the Temple in reparation for my sins. Yesterday at the Temple I shared my plan with the high priest. To my dismay he refused me. "We cannot accept your gifts because you have begotten no children for the nation."

Depressed, I read again the biblical story of Abraham and Sara who reached old age without children. And then God blessed them with a son, Isaac. Could not God do that for Anne and me? I left my wife and went to the desert. I fasted and prayed there for many weeks. Prayer became my food and drink. I begged God for a baby.

My wife, Anne, was also sad and ashamed of her infertile womb. Because of this she dressed like a widow. As she thought of me and my long retreat, she set aside her mourning clothes. She bathed herself, put on some perfume and dressed again like a young bride. Cheered by her transformation she went to our garden and sat under a laurel tree.

She mused to herself. "Why can't I be like the birds who multiply so abundantly? Even the sheep have lots of lambs. The waters in this brook gush merrily with lots of fish. Our vines are heavy with grapes and our farms white with wheat. Dear Lord, can't you give me a child?"

Then an angel came to Anne and said, "God has heard your prayer. You will soon have a baby." That same angel also appeared to me, Joachim, and brought me the good news. My prayer was heard.

Joyful, I proceeded immediately to the Temple to praise God. I brought ten lambs as an offering to God and some gifts for the priests. I donated several flocks of sheep to the poor. Anne met me at the golden gate of the Temple. She looked as radiant as a young bride.

Nine months later, my wife gave birth to a baby girl. We named her Mary. When our Mary was six months old we playfully urged her to walk. She stood up and walked seven steps toward us. Anne said, "Now you shall walk no more until we bring you to the Temple."

On Mary's first birthday, Anne and I hosted a banquet for our family and friends and the leading priests. Then we brought Mary to the Temple to present her to the Lord. We thanked God for our precious child.

When Mary was three, we brought her to live in the Temple. We hired virgins to light candles each day and to pray that Mary would never be tempted to leave God's Temple. The priest took Mary and kissed her and said that God had a special plan for her. He placed her on the third step of the altar. God filled Mary with grace and she danced for joy. Everyone loved her. Mary was nourished in the Temple like a dove and received food from the hands of an angel.

When Mary was twelve, the priests met to plan her
marriage. They appointed the high priest to enter the
Holy of Holies and pray for guidance. An angel came to
him and told him to order all the local widowers to
offer themselves as potential husbands. Each man was
to bring a rod. The man who received a miraculous sign
would be Mary's husband.

Among the candidates was a carpenter named
Joseph. The priest took all the rods and prayed for
enlightenment. Then he returned all the rods to the
owners. When Joseph received his rod, a dove came out
of it and rested on his head. The priest said, "God has
chosen you to be Mary's husband."

Joseph protested, "I already have sons. I am old.
She is but a girl. People will laugh at me." The priest
warned Joseph not to rebel against the Lord's evident
will. "Fear God and take Mary as your wife." Joseph
took Mary home. He told her, "I must go away for a
time building houses. God will look after you while I
am gone."

Four years passed. One day, an angel appeared to
Mary and said, "Hail, highly favored one. Do not fear.
You have found grace with God and shall conceive of
his Word." Mary said, "Shall I conceive as every woman
bears?" "Not so, Mary, for the power of the Lord shall
overshadow you." And Mary said, "Behold the
handmaid of the Lord. Be it so according to your word."

Day by day her womb grew. Mary was afraid and
hid herself in her home. She was sixteen when these
things happened. When Joseph returned, he was
shocked to see that his wife was pregnant. He was filled
with guilt and blamed himself. "I accepted Mary as a
virgin from the Temple and have not protected her
virginity. Who deceived me? Who came into my home
and defiled Mary?"

Joseph asked Mary, "Why have you done this?
How could you abandon your virginity after years in
the Temple and being fed by an angel?" Mary wept in
silence.

Joseph went out to think this over. "What shall I do
with her? I will put her away secretly." Then an angel

came to Joseph in a dream. "Don't worry. The Holy Spirit is the origin of your child. It will be a boy and you shall name him Jesus. He shall save people from their sins." Joseph was relieved and adored God for this grace. He watched lovingly over Mary.

I, Joachim, watched with sorrow when the priests discovered Mary's pregnancy, arrested the couple and ordered them to appear in court. Acting as prosecutor, one of the priests demanded, "How could you have done this?" Mary replied, "As God knows, I am pure and know not man." Turning to Joseph he asked, "Why have you done this?" Joseph declared, "God is my witness. I am pure concerning her." The priest rejected their testimony. And Joseph and Mary were silent.

The priest then ordered both of them to drink water which had been mixed with ink and dust from the Temple floor. If they became sick it was considered proof that they were lying. Joseph and Mary took the cups and drank the bitter water but it had no effect on them. The priest said, "If the Lord has not condemned you, neither do I." He released them and the happy couple went home.

Now came the decree of Augustus that a census should be taken of all the people. Joseph saddled the donkey and sat Mary on it. They set out for Bethlehem. One of his sons led the animal and Joseph followed. Some miles into the journey, Joseph noticed Mary's pained face. Mary said, "Joseph, take me down. The child within me presses to be born."

Joseph found a cave and led her into it. He left her in the care of his son and went to seek a midwife. While engaged in the search, he looked up at the heavens. Everything seemed utterly still. He was given a vision of the earth. All peoples paused from what they were doing and looked heavenward. Sheep stood still and would not move even when the shepherd raised his staff to poke them forward. The world stood still, for Jesus was coming into the world.

Joseph finally contacted a midwife, who agreed to come and help with the birth. As they came to the cave they saw a shining cloud over it. The cave itself was filled with so much light that neither Joseph nor the midwife could see Mary and the child until it receded. The midwife stayed a few days to care for Mary and the child.

On the twelfth night the little family was visited by wise men from the East. They told the parents about how they were guided by a star to Judea. They consulted King Herod and the Temple priests who used a prophecy from Micah 5:1 that the newborn king would be born in Bethlehem. The star then led them to this cave. They adored Jesus and left him gifts of gold, frankincense and myrrh and returned home by a different route.

The angered Herod ordered all children under two years of age to be killed. Joseph and Mary hid their child and kept him safe. Elizabeth fled with her son, John, to the mountains and protected him. Zechariah, John's father, was martyred by Herod for refusing to disclose the whereabouts of his son.

The priests replaced Zechariah with Simeon to whom the Holy Spirit said that he would not die until he saw the Messiah in the flesh.

I, Joachim, hope you liked this story about Mary and Joseph and how Jesus was born. It was written down by a man named James who closed his book with these words: "I will praise the Lord, who gave me the wisdom to write this history. Peace be to him who wrote and to him who reads."

Now that you have heard the story, you rightly may wonder how it fits into our study of Mary. For starters, it shows how early in Christian history (c. A.D. 150) there was a popular interest in Mary. It was clearly influenced by the Gospels, but has additional biographical material: Mary is a descendant of David; her parents are named Joachim and Anne; they receive their child as an answer to their prayers; Joseph is an old widower with children; he is selected for her by a miracle; there is a strong emphasis on Mary's virginal conception of Jesus.

Three Marian feasts can be traced to this story: Her

Conception, Her Birth, Her Presentation in the Temple. The liturgical feasts of Joachim and Anne also derive from this narrative. Mary's presentation in the Temple, with its colorful details, emphasizes the holiness of Mary. By inspiring the feast, it influenced centuries of meditation on Mary and generated numerous homilies about her in the Eastern Church.

One scholar comments on the literary beauty of the text in this way:

> In comparison with later infancy gospels the work has great merit. The borrowing of legendary details...is comparatively restrained. The whole presentation is impressive and extremely graphic and is evidence of a sober, sincere and poetic mind. The author, in using sources from oral and literary Christian tradition, besides much material from the Old Testament, especially the story of Samuel, knew how to form from them an artistic whole.
> —*Oscar Cullmann*, New Testament Apocrypha

The New Eve

In 1958 the German sculptor, Toni Zanz, created a metal door for the rebuilt church of St. Alban in Cologne. In the lower left of the door he placed Adam and Eve at the moment of the fall. In the upper right he situated the Second Adam and the Second Eve at the moment of crucifixion and redemption. This artist's choice can be traced back to a faith development in the second century.

James wrote his biography of Mary in A.D. 150. Around A.D. 190, Irenaeus, bishop of Lyons, developed his famous comparison of Eve and Mary in his treatise, *Against Heresies*. Thus the second century witnessed two influential works that included Mary as an essential presence.

To appreciate the importance of the insight of Irenaeus, we need to know that the first heresy faced by the Church was the denial of the humanity of Jesus. The sponsors of the heresy were called Gnostics and Docetists. They were so anxious to preserve their faith in Christ's divinity that they began to shield themselves from his real humanity. The Docetists (from the Greek *dokein*, to seem) said that Jesus just "seemed" human.

They used Paul's comparison of Adam and Christ as described in the New Testament to contrast Jesus as the man from heaven over against the merely human Adam. "Just as through one person (Adam) sin entered the world, and through sin, death...how much more will those who receive the abundance of grace...come to reign in life through the one person, Jesus Christ" (Romans 5:12, 17). They linked this text with: "The first man, Adam, became a living being, the last Adam a life-giving spirit.... The first man was from the earth, earthly; the second man, from heaven" (1 Corinthians 15:45,47).

They became so preoccupied with preserving the "man from heaven," that is, Jesus as divine, that they wanted to protect him from any of the problems of the flesh or being human. This was especially true about the most human moments in anyone's life—being born and dying. They determined to distance Jesus from birth and death—experiences they found irreconcilable with the divine.

They drove a wedge between the earthly Adam and the second Adam "from heaven." They found it hard to think of Jesus as really eating and drinking. And the events of Bethlehem (born of a virgin) and Calvary (suffering and death on the cross) offended them even more.

They believed a "man from heaven" could not really endure these human experiences. He only "seemed" to. Suffering and death were too human. It was unworthy of God. A famous Gnostic teacher, Basiledes, argued that when Simon of Cyrene carried Christ's cross, he was substituted for Jesus and was crucified in his stead. The cross was a stumbling block to these unbelievers.

Irenaeus devoted himself to countering this distortion of the New Testament teaching. He emphasized Christ's real humanity by invoking his real human birth from the virgin Mary. And going one step further, he introduced the comparison of the disobedience of the all-too-human virgin Eve, with the obedience of the evidently human virgin Mary.

He needed to introduce Mary into the discussion in order to defend the authentic humanity of Jesus. Moreover, he compared history's most famous two women who were no more than human, who were not from heaven, but from the earth. Both women acted freely and humanly. The devil did not force Eve. God did not force Mary, the second Eve. With these ideas in mind we can now look at the actual, remarkable words of Irenaeus:

> And just as it was through a virgin who disobeyed (namely Eve) that mankind was stricken and fell and died, so too it was through the Virgin (Mary), who obeyed the word of God, that mankind, resuscitated by life, received life. For the Lord (Christ) came to seek back the lost sheep, and it was mankind that was lost, and therefore he did not become some other formation, but he likewise, of her that was descended from Adam (namely, Mary), preserved the likeness of formation; for Adam had necessarily to be restored in Christ, that mortality be absorbed in immortality. And Eve (had necessarily to be restored) in Mary, that a virgin, by becoming an advocate of a virgin, should undo and destroy virginal disobedience by virginal obedience.
>
> —*Irenaeus of Lyons*, Proof of the Apostolic Preaching
> (*quoted in Pelikan*, Mary Through the Centuries)

Irenaeus was telling the Gnostics that salvation depended on a Christ who was human in his life and death. If Jesus is human he had to be really born. His mother had to be truly and completely human. Mary's obedience undid the disobedience of Eve. Mary's free obedience made her the second Eve and the guarantee of Christ's real humanity.

His argument involves a way of interpreting history. Everyone has heard such sayings: "History repeats itself." "History is a wheel." "We keep making the same mistakes." "There is nothing new under the sun." This idea that history is a story of endless repetitions is called the cyclical theory of history.

Irenaeus agreed that there are patterns in history that are repeated. But he argued that is not the whole story. He taught that there is also a "recapitulation" in history. The word comes from Latin and literally means "re-heads." It implies a radical restarting of history itself. Adam and Eve are not continually recreated. They do not yield to the tempter over and over. They are not repeatedly driven from paradise.

A decisive, second Adam came in Christ who repaired the damage done by the first Adam. A second Eve came in the person of the Virgin Mary. She undid and destroyed the virginal disobedience of Eve by her virginal obedience.

Saint Augustine explains this more fully. History is partly a wheel because people do commit the same old sins and also show the admirable qualities of courage and virtue. History does repeat itself. But history is also a "line," a process that is journeying toward a goal and a purpose. This means there are and can be "unrepeatable" events and persons.

They are the turning points of history. There *can* be something new under the sun. None have been more so than Jesus and Mary, the new Adam and the Second Eve. They "recapitulate," re-head, restart history. Jesus is the redeemer indeed—but at the human level, the responsible, free act of Mary is an essential part of the recapitulation.

Now we can see that even in the second century the role of Mary in the salvation story is seen as essential. She is a central figure in the Church's dispute with those who were unable to accept Jesus as fully human. The creeds of the Church always use historical moments to affirm Christ's humanity. The creeds state that Jesus was "born of the Virgin Mary" and suffered under Pontius Pilate. Historical figures—Mary and Pilate—are associated with Christ's birth and death, the most human of events.

None of this excludes faith in Christ's divinity. We will be dealing with this in the next chapter when we consider

Mary as the Mother of God.

The idea of the second Eve was imported to the Latin West where it inspired poetic symmetry and plays on words. The greeting of the angel, *Ave*, reversed the curse of Eve. The eighth-century hymn, "*Ave Maris Stella*," written for the feast of the Annunciation, playfully includes this reversal.

> *Sumens illud Ave*, Receiving that Ave
> *Gabrielis ore*, From the lips of Gabriel,
> *Funda nos in pace*, Establish us in peace,
> *Mutans nomen Hevae*, Changing Eva's name.

What are some lessons to be taken from the theme of Mary as the New Eve?

Mary's Humanity Ensures Jesus' Humanity. We need to take the incarnation seriously. The Son of God became a man. God is not revolted by humanity. God loved the world so much that he sent the Word to become flesh so we could be saved from sin and have divine life. God chose a human mother to give birth to his only Son. Jesus was born of the bone and blood of Mary, by the power of the Holy Spirit. The humanity of Mary helps us have faith in the humanity of Jesus. Nothing truly human is alien to God.

Covenant Is a Dialogue Between God and Humans. We praise Mary as the ark of the covenant. She shows us how covenant includes the partnership of a saving God and a responsible human being. Covenant is a relationship that takes place in history between God and humanity. God is active in our history to bring us salvation. Humans are meant to enter this process by responsible faith and obedience. Mary led the way by her responsive obedience to the call of God to consent to the birth of Jesus.

"When the fullness of time had come, God sent his Son, born of a woman, born under the law, to ransom those under the law, so that we might receive adoption"

(Galatians 4:4). Mary's human, free *fiat* was a necessary part of this event. Of course Mary was assisted by grace to obey, just as our obedience is aided by divine help. That does not diminish the humanity of her act or ours. In fact grace, in a mysterious manner, is designed to enable us to act most humanly and freely. God honored her humanity and honors ours, too, in the covenant union.

Mary and Jesus Exemplify Human Dignity. Vatican II teaches that Jesus revealed to us what it really means to be human. "It is only in the mystery of the Word made flesh that the mystery of man becomes clear. For Adam, the first man, was a type of him who was to come. Christ the Lord, Christ the new Adam, in the very revelation of the mystery of the Father and his love, fully reveals man to himself and brings to light his most high calling" (*The Church in the Modern World*).

Through her motherhood of Jesus, Mary assures us that Jesus is human. Mary connects Jesus to the human race. In turn Jesus, by assuming our humanity, fully exemplifies and reveals what we are meant to be and how great a dignity we possess. Here is the source of our calling to treat ourselves and every person with respect, reverence and honor.

Our self-worth and self-esteem are intimately tied to our identity with Jesus. This is an awareness that should grow each day over a lifetime. Mary lived with the mystery of Jesus for many years at Nazareth. She went before us in faith and in this endeavor. We must follow. Consider the Christmas homily of Saint Leo, "Christian, remember your dignity.... Bear in mind who is your head and of whose body you are a member" (Saint Leo the Great, Pope, *Liturgy of the Hours*).

Reflection

Remember the story of the *Book of James* and its significance for the early Church; recall the central role Mary played in countering the Gnostic/Docetist heresy.

* *Why do you think it is important to note that these developments about Mary already occurred in the second century?*

* *Think of three forms of dehumanization going on in our culture. How does Mary's human involvement in the plan of salvation inspire you to struggle for human dignity?*

* *We believe Jesus is both human and divine. Why should we be careful to maintain our belief in Christ's humanity?*

The *Book of James* is an apocryphal story. It is not part of sacred Scripture. Yet it has had an influence on creating liturgical feasts of Mary, Joachim and Anne. It has also inspired numerous works of art.

* *Review the story of Joachim, retold from the* Book of James *in this chapter. Which details are clearly legendary? What do they add or detract from the story of Mary?*

* *What are some contemporary works of creative imagination that treat of the lives of Jesus, Mary and other people of the Bible? What have you found of value in them?*

* *If you were to create a contemporary story of Mary, based on the scriptural narrative, what would you want to add to fill in unrecorded details? What principles would govern your choice?*

Our covenant union with God is a daily dialogue between God's merciful and saving presence in history and our free, responsible, faith response to God's love for us.

* *What is there in the life of Mary that will help us to sustain our covenant responsibilities?*

✳ *Why does the emphasis on our human response to salvation need such attention? Why does it not preclude faith or grace?*

✳ *What people do you know whose devotion to Mary illustrate a true faith linked with a genuine humanity?*

Prayer

Loving Father, in your divine plan to save us from sin and give us divine life, you sent your Son to be born of the Virgin Mary. Because of her Jesus could be truly human. You also called Mary to a free act of faith and obedience to consent to this gift of love. By your will Mary's obedience undid the disobedience of Eve, making Mary the New Eve. We praise you for these graces and pray that Mary's intercession with your Son will help us appreciate our human dignity as well as grace us to act humanly, freely and obediently in our covenant with you. Amen.

William Blake
THE NATIVITY
c. 1799
Philadelphia Museum of Art
Gift of Mrs. William T. Tonner

CHAPTER FOUR

❀

Mother of God

Mother dear, remember me,

And never cease your care,

Till in heaven eternally,

Your love and bliss I share.

My God, My Son

I'm here in the stable beside Mary and I'm right inside the Gospel and the Gospel is saying, "And she gave birth to her firstborn" (Luke 2:7).

Transcendence has become incarnate, fear has become sweetness, I put my arms around incommunicability.

Distance has become closeness. God has become a son.

Do you understand the reversal that has taken place?

For the first time a woman could say with truth, "My God, my son."

So now I am no longer frightened. If God is that baby lying on the straw in the cave, God cannot frighten me.

And if I can whisper, "My God, my son," sitting beside Mary, then paradise has come into my home and I am truly at peace.

I can be afraid of my father, yes, especially if I don't really know him; but of my son, never.

Of my son whom I hold in my arms, whom I cradle at my breast; of my son who asks me for protection and warmth, oh no.

I cannot be afraid.

I cannot be afraid.

I cannot be afraid any more. Peace, which is the absence of fear, abides in me.

Now the only task that remains to me is to believe.

And believing is like generating. In faith I continue to generate Christ as son.

This is what Mary did. It was easy enough for her to generate Jesus in the flesh: nine months were enough.

But to generate, to give birth to Jesus in faith—for that she needed her whole life from Bethlehem to Calvary.

—*Carlo Carretto*, Blessed Are You Who Believed

Carlo Caretto has spent many years in the North African desert with the Little Brothers of Jesus, devoted to prayer and contemplation. Learning the fate of a Taureg girl—killed because she was found to be pregnant before her marriage—opened his eyes to the real life Mary must have led in Nazareth, where she would have been subject to her neighbors' scrutiny.

He does not consider Mary a remote figure, but rather the "sister of his heart." She accompanies him on his own faith pilgrimage. In his startling insight, he contrasts the nine months it took for Mary to become God's mother in the flesh to the lifetime it took to generate Jesus in faith. For thirty-three years and beyond, Mary probed in silence the mystery of the Lord Jesus, of whom she knew she alone could say, "My God, my son."

It was at Ephesus that the Church formally declared that Mary was truly the mother of God. There is a simple shrine on a mountain overlooking that ancient city. It is called the House of Mary. Tradition holds that Saint John heeded the wish of Jesus at the cross that he take care of Mary. "And from that hour the disciple took her into his home" (John 19:27). This tradition claims that John went to Ephesus to exercise his apostolic ministry and brought Mary with him to a modest home there.

Archaeologists have excavated the site and restored the small stone building, which today has two rooms. The larger serves as a chapel and the smaller contains a page from the Koran, speaking of the honor given Mary by the Muslims. Outside the house is a little park and an altar for outdoor Masses. Simplicity and understatement characterize this shrine. It is not a place frequented by crowds, but rather by a quiet, steady stream of pilgrims who come to rest, think and pray in union with Mary.

Rarely is the mystery of Mary more aptly captured. This unassuming shrine at Ephesus takes the mighty doctrine of Mary as mother of God and makes it accessible. The House of Mary is restful, inclining visitors to unhurried prayer. But the city it overlooks was once anything but restful, back in the time of the events that led to the Council of Ephesus and the declaration of Mary as *Theotokos*, the God-bearer.

Struggle in the Early Church

Previously, we examined the reason we call Mary the new Eve. When the Church Fathers were struggling against a heretical challenge that denied the humanity of Jesus, they emphasized that Jesus was born of the blood and bone of Mary. Jesus took his human nature from her. He was authentically human because he was truly born of Mary, a human mother.

But in the fourth and fifth centuries A.D., the second great heresy emerged. It was called Arianism, named after its founder, Arius. He was an Alexandrian priest who claimed that Jesus was only a creature and not the divine Son of God. Arius could not believe that God would become united with human flesh, with human nature. That would debase divinity.

Arius devised a new way to describe Jesus. First, God created a superior, perfect creature called the *Logos*—the Word. Then God proceeded to make all other creatures through this Logos. Finally, God made it possible for this Logos to become a human, born of a woman. In this new form the Logos assumed an imperfect status and proceeded to make progress in perfection. By God's will his death was redemptive. In this way he saved us and was promoted to his perfect life once more.

As you can see, Arius could not accept the teaching of John's Gospel: "In the beginning was the Word (Logos)...and the Word was God.... And the Word became flesh..." (John 1:1,14). Denying John's Gospel, Arius argued that the Word was not God. The Word was a creature, albeit a perfect and impressive one. Somehow, Arius got it into his head that the incarnation of the Son of God in the womb of the Virgin Mary was impossible.

This should not surprise us today since millions do not

believe Jesus was divine. It is true that a billion Christians have faith in Jesus as Son of God, but a billion Muslims do not, nor do countless others. It is, after all, a matter of faith.

Arius persuaded thousands of people, including many bishops, to abandon the ancient faith and accept his novel teaching. He was a captivating communicator and propagandist. He created songs to embed his new teachings in the minds of the masses. He made his doctrine sound appealing by implying that God would never contaminate his glory by being united to the problems of human flesh and nature. God was too beautiful and perfect for that.

The first four councils of the Church—Nicea, First Constantinople, Ephesus and Chalcedon—battled the Arian heresy and illumined the mysteries of the Trinity and the Incarnation in a way that has been a theological benchmark for the Church ever since. Still, so powerful was Arianism that it lasted for nearly four centuries before dying out.

Saint Athanasius, the bishop of Alexandria, vigorously fought the teachings of Arius. From his arsenal of arguments, Athanasius invoked a title for Mary that was instrumental in clarifying the truth about our Lord Jesus. That title was *Theotokos*, Greek for "God-bearer." Just as Mary had been instrumental in understanding Christ as really human, so now she would be essential for the Church's faith that Jesus was really divine—truly Lord.

Popular devotion in the Alexandrian Church of the fourth century had begun to use the title Theotokos for Mary. It became more than a devotional title when it was connected to the feast of the "Commemoration of Mary." This liturgical celebration was held on the Sunday after Christmas and it was meant to honor Mary's birth into heavenly joy.

Athanasius used this feast to support his argument for Christ's divinity. There is an axiom in the Church that says "The law of praying is the law of believing" (*Lex orandi, lex credendi*). It means that when the Church celebrates a teaching in her liturgical prayer it treats that teaching as a matter of faith. We pray what we believe, and vice versa.

When Alexandrian Christians celebrated the liturgy of the Commemoration of Mary they spoke of her as Theotokos. Athanasius could point to this feast as one of his arguments that Jesus was divine. Mary is the God-bearer, not just the bearer of a created Logos as Arius contended. The Council of Nicea in A.D. 325 agreed with Athanasius and taught that the Lord Jesus was divine, having the same divine nature as the Father.

The Conflict Over Theotokos

In this next section I will ask your patience as we wade into some dense theological waters that were the meat and potatoes of a struggle to understand how the divine and the human were connected in Christ. We will see once again that a proper understanding of Mary helped people grasp the real meaning of Christ. This will not be an easy journey for us. Nor was it for the Fathers of the fifth century. But our history is a record of our faith development.

Understandably you may be tempted to say, "These are not modern questions. I don't have these problems." But in fact these old questions have arisen in new forms. Just think of the rash of cover stories in the news weeklies— *Time, Newsweek, U.S. News and World Report*—about the Jesus Seminar whose academic focus considers the historical accuracy of the Gospels. This is an eclectic group of Scripture scholars who hope to determine the credibility of the Gospels—the essential sources of our faith in Christ. Coffee tables across America have been strewn with their findings which cast doubt on Christ's resurrection, divine origin and saving work. This popularization of heresy is as old as Arius and the Gnostics.

We will not take time here to attempt to refute these new faith challenges; rather, we will consider the courage and imagination of those who faced similar challenges in the past. The more carefully we consider our past, the more confidently we can approach our future. We are not the first to face faith dilemmas, nor will we be the last. But this exercise will help us see how Mary's role is often the key to explaining the Church's understanding of Christ.

Over a century after Athanasius, a priest named Nestorius became the new Patriarch-Bishop of Constantinople (present-day Istanbul, Turkey). The city had become the glittering capitol of the Eastern Empire. Its emperors commanded vast territories. Its patriarchs shared in the prestige of the imperial city and exercised enormous influence in the Church.

While the pope in Rome retained ultimate authority on Church teaching, the patriarchs of three Eastern churches— Constantinople, Antioch and Alexandria—were major players in clarifying Church teachings, especially when heresies arose.

Antioch, in Syria, was the oldest and most venerated church of the East after Jerusalem. In New Testament times it had become the center of Christianity after the destruction of Jerusalem in A.D. 70. It was from Antioch the mission to the gentiles took place. By the fifth century it was a leading theological center as well. It produced outstanding theologians such as Ephrem and John of Damascus. They leaned toward a rational study of the Bible, using grammar and history in their interpretations.

Alexandria, in Egypt, had become a prominent church in a wealthy trading city. Egyptian monasticism, led by Saint Anthony, had created armies of monks in the nearby desert who inspired a lively faith among the people. Alexandria was also a theological center whose thinkers used poetry and allegory to interpret scripture. It boasted of a succession of brilliant theologians such as Clement, Origen, Athanasius and Cyril, who tended to explore spiritual understandings of the Bible.

The major issue facing the Church of these years was the proper understanding of Jesus Christ as both God and man. Arius had claimed he was not God. The Church at the Council of Nicea reaffirmed Jesus was divine.

The next debate considered how the divine and human

were linked in Christ. Nicea had solved one problem, only to introduce a new one.

Bishop Cyril of Alexandria stressed the union of the divinity and humanity. He wanted to protect Christ's divinity from being denied. He taught that the divine nature penetrated the human nature of Christ as a fire permeates a log. He failed to see that this picture was like a blender that dissolved the two natures so that each lost its independent reality. Christ's humanity is lost in the process.

Diodorus of Antioch was more interested in the separate identity of the divine and human in Christ. He wanted to protect Christ's humanity from being overwhelmed by divinity. So he spoke of the link between the human and the divine as a moral union and not an essential one. He failed to see that he was making the union so thin that it would be easy to separate them altogether.

Cyril made the union so close that the parts disappeared. He believed his solution best defended Christ's divinity. Diodorus made the union so tentative that the parts need not stay united. He believed his solution best defended Christ's humanity. Both were well-intentioned men of faith, agonizing over a theological truth in a state of development.

Now comes the third partner in the discussion, Nestorius of Constantinople. His spiritual heritage came from the Antioch school where he was trained. He was inclined to save Christ's humanity from being lost in the divinity. He tended to separate the two very much like Diodorus.

But it led him to go too far. He noticed that his people were increasingly fond of calling Mary *Theotokos*. He feared this would threaten faith in the real humanity of Jesus. In addition he could not see how Mary could be the mother of God. A human being could not generate divinity. His teacher at Antioch had convinced him to teach that Mary was only the *Christotokos*, the Christ-bearer.

To make this argument work, he would have to say that Mary is the mother of the purely human Jesus who had both a human nature and a human person. After his birth the divine person and divine nature of the Son of God was united to her son. Now we have a case of Christ having two persons and two natures.

It might help here to describe what is meant by *nature* and *person*. A person is a who, the source of responsibility. The person answers the question, "Who did it?" A nature is a what, the agent that performed the act. Nature answers the question, "What did it?" In a murder mystery the detective may conclude that the victim was killed by a member of the household (the what, a human). He then goes on to discover that Bernard the butler did it (the who, a person).

In Jesus there are two natures. In his humanity he thinks like a human being, hungers and aches like a human, dies like a human. In his divine nature he performs like a God doing miracles and redeeming the world. But there is only one person, a divine *who* that is responsible for all these acts.

That is what Nestorius failed to see.

In trying to save Christ's humanity, he gave him a human person as well as a divine one. Nestorius created a faith crisis in the fifth-century Church. When one of the Church's most important bishops gave a novel meaning to Mary's title, Theotokos, and introduced a human person into the meaning of Jesus Christ, a major response was needed. That reply occurred at the Council of Ephesus in 431.

The Council of Ephesus

The disturbing news of the rejection of Theotokos by Nestorius reached Pope Celestine I. On August 11, 430, he held a meeting to deal with this problem. He commissioned Bishop Cyril of Alexandria to take leadership in resolving this issue. Since it had become customary for the emperor of the Eastern Empire to convene the ecumenical councils, it fell to Theodosius II to summon a council to be held at Ephesus.

Among the great bishop-theologians invited to the Council was the prince of theology, Augustine of Hippo in North Africa. But he died on August 28, 430, while the Vandals were besieging his city.

The date for the opening of the Council was set for June 7, 431.

The City. If tradition is correct that Saint John brought our Blessed Mother with him to Ephesus, they would have probably sailed north on the Aegean Sea to the southern part of what is present-day Turkey. Ephesus was five miles inland and connected to the sea by an inlet that needed constant dredging to remain navigable.

Arriving at the wharf they would have seen the fourth largest city of the Roman Empire. It was surrounded by mountains on three sides. Over two hundred thousand people lived there. The poor occupied the mountainsides, while the rich lived in the city itself. Archaeologists have restored many of the classical buildings which they would have seen, such as the Library of Celsus.

Occupying a huge space at the time was the temple of Artemis, goddess of fertility. It was so splendid that it was considered to be one of the Seven Wonders of the Ancient World. (Today only one pillar remains.) Resting on a marble platform over four hundred feet long, the temple covered an area as large as a football field. Over a hundred marble columns rose to the height of a five-story building. Sculptures, paintings and gold plate adorned its walls. In the center of the temple was a sacred stone that "fell from the sky"—most likely a meteorite.

The temple housed a statue of Artemis, the fertility goddess of Asia Minor. Mary could not have missed seeing the many little silver statues of Artemis on sale throughout the city. The statues represented the goddess as a many-breasted figure, wearing a crown decorated with the signs of the seasons. The purchaser would place the little statue in the temple and provide an endowment to keep the image clean. On the goddess's birthday these images would be paraded through the city to the outdoor theater for a celebration.

The irony cannot be lost on us: Mary, the fruitful spiritual mother of Christians moved to a home overlooking a city that worshipped a pagan fertility goddess.

Had she been granted a vision of the future and seen in detail June 7, 431, she would have seen a ship arrive with Cyril of Alexandria and the Egyptian bishops. Perhaps a few hours later she would have noted the arrival of Nestorius and his entourage from Constantinople. He immediately went into seclusion, with imperial guards to protect him, until his bishop friends from Syria came. Bishop John of Antioch and the Syrian bishops did not come until June 26. Not until early July did the delegation from Pope Celestine disembark at Ephesus. Assorted bishops from other places in the East were also present.

I think Mary would certainly have smiled at the outcome of the council. I hesitate to imagine what she might have thought about the process that led to its resolution. Our faith holds that the Holy Spirit presides over an ecumenical council, but this does not eliminate the human limitations of the participants or the use of outside pressures to determine its progress.

For those who can recall Vatican II, we need to think only of the effort of the media to shape its decisions and the sharp discussions that took place at the sessions themselves. Councils are often stormy, even if the truths that come from them are peaceful and enduring. As we shall now see, the proceedings at Ephesus were equally awkward at times.

The Council. All in all, two hundred bishops eventually assembled in Ephesus. Political pressures and human passions complicated the theological discussions. Two weeks passed after Patriarch Cyril and the Egyptian bishops arrived, and still no one else was there except Nestorius who refused to attend until the Antioch delegation came.

Cyril waited impatiently for the other bishops and the

papal legates to arrive. Knowing he possessed authority from Pope Celestine I to preside at the Council, he finally decided to convene the Council without them and opened the proceedings on June 22. Since he and the Egyptian bishops were of one mind, having long before discussed the issue in depth and having determined to defend Mary as Theotokos, they did not take long to proclaim their decision officially.

A bishop read passages from Cyril's letters to Nestorius in which he defended his position on the Theotokos. The following quote from Cyril can give you some feeling for what he had to say:

> For the very reason that the holy Virgin gave fleshly birth to God substantially united with flesh we declare her to be "Mother of God," not because the Word's nature somehow derived its origin from flesh...but because, as we previously affirmed, he substantially united humanity with himself, and underwent fleshly birth from her womb... These are the views we have been taught to hold both by the holy apostles and evangelists and by inspired Scripture in its entirety and from the true confession of the blessed fathers.
> —*Cyril of Alexandria*, Third Letter to Nestorius

Notice in the last sentence that Cyril links his explanation with the faith of the Church from the time of the apostles. He rejects the teaching of Nestorius that Mary just bore a human person and God later provided the divine person. Mary is mother of the one person, Jesus, who is Lord and God. Jesus is the Son of God. Mary is his mother. Therefore, Mary is mother of God.

Cyril makes it clear that Mary is not the origin of the divine nature. The Son of God pre-existed Mary from all eternity. The Son of God willed to be substantially united to the child that Mary bore in the flesh. Hence there are not two persons, a human and divine one, but one person, God's only Son. Mary generated Jesus who is Lord-God in the flesh.

Apparently the bishops on that day did not linger over the matter or debate it at length. They had gone through that process at length back in Egypt. By the end of that day they accepted the doctrine of Theotokos as explained by Cyril. He praised the Council's decision as a victory of the Lord over the enemies of the faith. Since the church at Ephesus was pro-Theotokos, there was great rejoicing at the conciliar outcome. It was reported that a rousing march of Christians, carrying flaming torches, coursed through the city singing praises to Mary as the Theotokos.

But that was only the beginning of a longer process.

Bishop John of Antioch and the Syrian bishops arrived four days later on June 26. They were angered by the news that Cyril had convened the Council without them. They re-opened the Council and rejected "Cyril's Council," and even deposed him as bishop. Actually they were not opposed in principle to the doctrine of Theotokos, but they believed that Cyril's explanation was insufficient and they were irritated by his arbitrary manner.

The Council of Ephesus was in stalemate, but not about Theotokos. That was an agreed title for Mary. The impasse rather was about an explanation acceptable to all.

In early July, the papal legates arrived. They met with Cyril and his bishops and approved their condemnation of the view of Nestorius that Mary was only the Christotokos, mother of Christ, not of God. They agreed there were not two persons in Christ. They censured John of Antioch and his bishops, excommunicating them—probably for their intemperate behavior and possibly due to a suspicion about their orthodoxy.

At the same time, the legates realized the language of the Council used by Cyril was not yet ready to be part of the Church's creed. They forbade any new formulas of faith other than the Nicene Creed.

In August the emperor Theodosius II felt he had to intervene to prevent religious chaos. He deposed Cyril and Nestorius and put them under house-arrest in Constantinople. At the insistence of Emperor Theodosius, for the next six weeks the remaining bishops went to Chalcedon, a town just across the Bosporus (a twenty-minute ride by today's ferry). There they engaged, unsuccessfully, in theological discussions meant to resolve the impasse.

Bishop John asked the emperor for amnesty for Nestorius and offered him refuge in Syria. Cyril, ever the activist, enlisted powerful support at the emperor's court by a shrewd distribution of gifts. In late September, 431, Theodosius formally closed the Council of Ephesus. With the help of important friends, Cyril escaped back to Alexandria. Nestorius retired to a monastery near Antioch.

Not until 433 was the matter of language explaining Theotokos finally resolved. The "Formula of Union" proposed by the Syrians was accepted by Cyril. Another building-block in our faith understanding of Christ and Mary was set in place. This formula is beautifully written and part of it is printed here as a subject for prayer and meditation.

> Accordingly, we acknowledge our Lord Jesus Christ, the only begotten Son of God, to be perfect God and perfect man made up of soul endowed with reason and of body, begotten of the Father before the ages in respect of his Godhead and the same born in the last days for us and for our salvation of Mary the Virgin in respect of his manhood, consubstantial with the Father in Godhead, consubstantial with us in manhood.
>
> A union of two natures has been effected and therefore we confess one Christ, one Son, one Lord. By virtue of this understanding of the union which involves no merging, we acknowledge the holy Virgin to be "Mother of God" because God the Word "became man" and united to himself the temple he took from her as a result of his conception.
>
> —*Translation by Lionel Wickham*

The story of the Council of Ephesus reveals a robust Church fighting its way through deposed and arrested bishops and excommunications to reach a consensus of faith in a critical doctrine about Christ and Mary. From our point of view, their strategies may seem extreme, too passionate, too ready to use heavy-handed sanctions.

But the participants in these dialogues also spent many hours and years in profound reflection on the mysteries they hoped to clarify as far as is possible in this world. Don't think that the turbulence of the council is the whole story. Read the volume of letters written by Cyril of Alexandria in order to appreciate the depth of faith, prayer and thinking he demonstrates.

On the other hand, we may need to question ourselves for being passive, laid-back or too inclined to let the issues slide by. Some of us would rather be polite than right. I do not suggest we should resort to the methods of the past. I do believe we need the passion for the truths of faith that motivated the bishops of that exciting era. In our time the cultural preference is to see everything in terms of the person, and this has been very beneficial for the faith.

But it ought not to exclude a passion for truth. Jesus was indeed the greatest individualist when he said, "I am the truth." This did not prevent him from also saying, "I *have* the truth," in the sense that he taught the truths of faith in the Sermon on the Mount, the parables, his wisdom sayings and many other places. The Church Fathers valued the personal, but they also prized the importance of accurate Church teachings. We are heirs to this precious tradition.

Conclusion

The emergence of popular devotion to Mary already occurred in Alexandria over a century before the Council of Ephesus. Long before these theological debates many Christians began saying the venerable prayer that addresses Mary as Theotokos and begs for her protection. We still say this prayer today. It is at least seventeen hundred years old.

> We fly to your patronage, O Holy Mother of God
> (Theotokos). Despise not our petitions in our necessities,
> but deliver us from all danger, O ever glorious and
> blessed Virgin.

The events at Ephesus opened up a universal devotion to Mary that had previously been practiced in some parts of the Church. Right after the Council, Pope Sixtus III built the most important shrine to Mary in the West, the basilica of St. Mary Major in Rome. Its mosaics of the annunciation and the epiphany provided artistic expressions of this truth about Mary.

From then on Mary would have a permanent place in the consciousness of the faithful. True, she was always present in the scriptural accounts. But now the significance of her role in the history of salvation would be seen even more clearly. Christians did not start with Mary. They began with Christ. It is on account of the Lord Jesus that Mary received special attention, not on account of herself.

It was Mary who gave Jesus his human nature. She gave him hands with which to bless children. She gave him the feet that went in search of lost sheep. Mary gave him the eyes that would weep over the loss of a close friend. Mary gave him the body that would die on the Cross for our salvation. She gave him the body that would be transformed into a risen body and would sacramentally become the Eucharist. By the will of God and her graced consent to the conception of Jesus, Mary is forever linked to the mysteries of Christ's incarnation, life, saving death and resurrection and presence in the Eucharist.

This was the faith intuition of ancient Christians, a faith that was officially confirmed at Ephesus. Believers understood that if Mary was Christ's mother, she could be their spiritual mother, too.

I have tried to show how important Mary as Theotokos is for a theological understanding of Christ. Mary is the mother of God. This is the doctrinal basis for our love for Mary as our mother, too, and our ardent intercessor with

Christ on our behalf. I have found that the closer we situate Mary within doctrine and liturgy the more intimately we are drawn to her and the more powerful is her ability to bring us nearer to Christ.

Now the second half of the Hail Mary makes a lot more sense, doesn't it?

Holy Mary, Mother of God, pray for us sinners, now and at the hour of our death. Amen.

Reflection

Cardinal Newman wrote a touching and remarkable comment about the impact of Mary's maternity. To Newman it was plain that Jesus was so close to Mary that he must even have physically looked like her.

> He imbibed, He absorbed into his divine Person, her blood and the substance of her flesh; by becoming man of her, He received her lineaments and features, as the appropriate character in which he was to manifest Himself to mankind. The child is like the parent, and we may well suppose that by His likeness to her was manifested her relationship to Him.
> —*Ian Ker*, Newman on Being a Christian

Mary passed on to Jesus his physical features, as Newman strikingly attests. Her motherhood went beyond that as she formed his human character. Mary trained and educated him as any mother brings up a child. Her virtues would have an impact on him. All of us realize that our mother's influence is recognizable in us and we can reasonably conclude that Mary's influence was evident in Jesus.

Mary was more than merely the biological mother of the Lord Jesus. Mary's task in the Incarnation was not over after the event in the stable at Bethlehem. Birth was followed by education. Mary exercised a continuous formation of the young Jesus as he grew from infancy to childhood to the teen years to young manhood.

The New Testament does not tell us how this happened. There is only one brief glimpse given by Luke 2:41-52 in the narrative of the losing and finding of the boy Jesus in the Temple. Mary acts like a typical mother, with the emotions of loss and anxiety and with the maternal demand to know why her son would go off without telling her and Joseph.

It is interesting that Luke cites her words and not Joseph's. "Son, why have you done this to us? Your father and I have been looking for you with great anxiety" (2:48). These are words we expect a mother to say. Mary is not shy about asserting her maternal authority. It flows from her love, of course. Why should she not have worried about him? The passage closes with words about Jesus continuing to grow in wisdom and grace before God and all others.

Aside from this brief anecdote, we know nothing else about what happened between mother and son all those years. Her maternal training style, her motherly witness of virtues, her approach to parenting is not recorded for us. Nonetheless, we should not forget that it happened. Mary was indeed mother of God. But she was also a human mother of a son who had a human upbringing, however that occurred.

I share this reflection with you because I believe that just as Mary knew how to be a mother of Jesus, she knows how to be our mother, too. She raised him in a household of faith. She had the remarkable experience of forming him in a human and spiritual sense while at the same time contemplating his mystery. How this happens is not revealed to us.

This should move us to be eager to have Mary offer us her maternal care. Ask Mary, as I do, to mother us in faith, hope and love of the Lord Jesus. When your heart is anxious, turn to Mary and say, "Mary, put my heart at peace." When your mind is too busy, look to Mary and pray, "Mary, settle down my mind." When you want to grow and deepen your life, look to Mary and beg, "Mary, just as you helped Jesus grow in wisdom and grace, help me also to advance on the spiritual path which God has laid out for me."

* *How can Mary help me deal with the demons and anxious moments that disturb my peace?*

* *How can Mary offer me the peace of mind to make my way through the moral challenges which I face each day?*

* *How can Mary form me as she formed Jesus in wisdom and grace and knowledge?*

* *What can I do to see that just as Mary was a real mother to Jesus, she can be a real mother to me?*

* *I know a man who lost his mother when he was seven. From that moment on he turned to Mary and adopted her as his mother. His direct act of faith is an example of what I can do as well.*

Prayer

Holy Mary, Mother of God, pray for me and form me in Christ. Amen.

OUR LADY OF CZESTOCHOWA

Icon, Jasna Gora Monastery
Czestochowa, Poland

CHAPTER FIVE

❃

Ever Virgin

Where troops of virgins follow the Lamb

Through streets of the golden city,

Who is she that walks, in the lily throng

Clothed with the sun... To the jewel pavement?...

The glory of virgins is she, a maiden mother....

—*Venantius Fortunatus (530-609),
Translation by Sister Maura*

Saint Ambrose's Royal Hall of Chastity

Ambrose's thought on virginity could be summed up in
one word: *integritas*. This meant the precious ability to
keep what was one's own untarnished by alien
intrusion.

For in what does the chastity of a virgin consist, but
in an integrity unexposed to taint from the outside? It
was because she had avoided all admixture that Mary
had been chosen by Christ as the source of his own
flesh. In a phrase heavy with late Roman meaning,
Mary was an *aula pudoris*, a royal hall of undamaged
chastity. Any inhabitant of Milan knew what that
meant. The imperial palace was a building rendered
perpetually sacred by the presence of the emperor. No
private citizen, at any time, could dare to occupy its
silent, golden halls. The body of Mary, and that of each
of her followers as consecrated virgins, was such a
hall....

Mary's womb stood for all that was unbroken and
sacred in the world. It was the "Gate of the sanctuary
which looks toward the East," of Ezekiel's vision of the
Temple. "The gate shall be shut, it shall not be opened,
and no man shall enter by it...because the Lord, the God
of Israel hath entered by it, and therefore it shall be
shut" (Ezekiel 42:2).

The ceremony of the *velatio*, of the solemn veiling of
consecrated virgins, was a fully public affair, celebrated
at a few high festivals of the year.... In a crowded
church, blazing with light and with the shimmer of
white, triumphal robes, a burst of rhythmic shouting
marked the moment when the consecrated woman took
up her position behind a special, pure white marble
railing that marked her off from the rest of the basilica
as clearly as did the chancel altar rail around the
sanctuary. Noble men and women would push through
the crowds to exchange with her the kiss of peace.

—*Peter Brown*, The Body and Society

Arguably, the Marian shrine of Czestochowa at Jasna Gora (White Mountain) in Poland is the place where Mary's virginity is most honored. In my two pilgrimages to this holy ground I experienced the mystery of her virginity as the promise of her undivided heart to God. I know that her icon is weighted with centuries of history, especially as it has figured so strongly in the saving of Poland from invaders.

I realize as well that the icon of Mary protected Polish identity, culture and language during the years of partition when Russia, Prussia, Austria—and later the Nazis and Communists—attempted to destroy them.

So, clearly Mary is their defender and protector. It is no accident they call her the "Queen of Poland." But it is her virginal aspect, that strong, pure sense of the undivided heart, that summarizes her impact on the Polish soul. A faith in the Lord Jesus that does not waver is captured by the virginal impulse.

It underlies the strength of character of those who look to Mary at Jansa Gora for inspiration. Pope John Paul II has left a bloodied sash from the assassination attempt at the base of Mary's icon. Lech Walesa has entrusted a memorial of his Nobel Peace Prize to the treasury at Jasna Gora. The beating heart of Mary as Virgin captivates Polish faith and identity as well as those of us who journey to her icon at the summit of White Mountain.

Now this is not a reflection on Mary's virginity apart from her being Mother of God. They belong essentially to each other. Mary's virginal *amen* to Gabriel led to the conception of Jesus. I am simply sharing with you the view of Mary which moved me most at White Mountain. And it is Mary's virginal witness which is the subject of our reflection in this chapter.

Peter Brown was a Fellow of All Souls College, Oxford, and is now a professor at Princeton University. We opened this chapter with a passage from his study of the growth of the virginal and celibate ideal from Paul to Augustine. He draws our attention to the fact that early Christianity emerges at the same time that the Roman culture of Late Antiquity is declining. Thoughtful pagans were revolted by perceived sexual excesses of the times. Reacting to this, they adopted ascetic practices which disciplined the body and idealized self-restraint.

The emperor, Marcus Aurelius, characterized life as a warfare against all undisciplined passions. He concluded that Philosophy will lift us above these rebellious emotions to a realm of detachment and inner peace. "To be a philosopher is to keep unsullied the divine spirit within him, so that it may transcend all pleasure and pain" (*Meditations*). In his view, the most dangerous enemy of chastity was softness of mind. Philosophy would create a muscular mind that could control the passions.

Early Christianity was equally interested in countering the sexual corruption of Late Antiquity. It is not surprising, then, that it would favor the growth of consecrated virginity and clerical celibacy. Christian ascetics could appeal to an athletic metaphor in the writings of Saint Paul to support a disciplined life-style and self-restraint.

Paul cited the example of a runner in a race who is temperate in all things so he can win the contest. He also uses the image of a boxer who does more than beat the air. "I drive my body and train it, for fear that, after having preached to others, I myself should be disqualified" (1 Corinthians 9:27).

In searching for role models, the Church Fathers turned to the perpetual virginity of Mary, a teaching of faith from the earliest years of Christianity. The virginal ideal, along with the means to achieve it, appealed to all those who would create an alternative life-style to the prevailing pagan one. Not everyone would choose virginity. But it was a powerful motivating model, since it encompassed the conquest of the unruly passions, a goal to which Christians of all kinds aspired.

Since Mary was an icon of purity, her image and example was a compelling one. However, before we try to see her exemplary influence on Christian life, we need to see how the doctrine of Mary's perpetual virginity developed.

Saint Augustine summarized the mystery of Mary's virginity in these words: "A virgin conceived. A virgin brought forth. A virgin remained" (Sermon). The Latin aphorism says that Mary was a virgin *"ante partum, in partu, post partum"*(before, in and after birth). All the Church Fathers, with the exception of Tertullian, agree to these three beliefs about Mary's virginity:

1. Mary conceived her Son, Jesus, while remaining a
   virgin.

2. Her virginity was not altered by childbirth.

3. She remained a virgin in her marriage with Joseph.

Each of these truths of faith deserve some comment.

A Virgin Conceives

Scripture confirms Mary's virginal conception of Jesus. The Christmas narratives of Matthew and Luke make the same claim: "Now the birth of Jesus the Messiah took place in this way. When his mother Mary had been engaged to Joseph, but before they lived together, she was found to be with child from the Holy Spirit" (Matthew 1:18).

> Mary said to the angel, "How can this be, since I am a
> virgin?" The angel said to her, "The Holy Spirit will
> come upon you, and the power of the Most High will
> overshadow you; therefore, the child to be born will be
> holy; he will be called Son of God" (Luke 1:34-35).

Matthew and Luke convey the following teachings:

Jesus was conceived by the Spirit. Joseph is only the legal father of Jesus. The conception happened while Mary and Joseph were betrothed. The birth occurred when they lived together. Jesus was born in Bethlehem during the reign of King Herod. After the birth (and temporary exile in Egypt), the family lived in Nazareth. The early Christian communities of Matthew and Luke and others clearly believed in the virginal conception of Jesus.

Some contemporary Scripture interpreters assert that the virgin birth story is only a symbolic way of expressing a theological truth that Jesus is Son of God. But Luke sounds like he is talking of facts, not symbols.

> "Since many have undertaken to set down an orderly account of the events that have been fulfilled among us, just as they were handed on to us by those who from the beginning were eyewitnesses and servants of the word, I too, have decided, after investigating everything carefully from the very first, to write an orderly account for you, most excellent Theophilus, so that you may know the truth concerning the things about which you have been instructed" (Luke 1:1-4).

Luke is writing for Greek readers who would expect facts. It is true that both Luke and Matthew weave into their narratives images from the Old Testament (such as the "Daughter of Zion" and the "cloud over the Tabernacle"), but these should be seen as helps for understanding the facts, not a subversion of them.

Another point to remember is that the virginal conception is essentially related to the Incarnation. The mystery of the Son of God becoming man is on the same level of faith as his Resurrection. We cannot have a symbol at the beginning and a reality at the end. The two mysteries are of the same quality and deserve the same depth of faith from us.

The birth is virginal. The Church's intuition of faith discerns Mary's retention of virginity in giving birth to Jesus. The Church does not definitively say how this is so, only that it is so. The Church Fathers tended to see the birthing event as a miracle, like light passing through a window, the emergence of Christ from a sealed tomb, his going through closed doors, the departure of the Word from the bosom of the Father. The medieval scholars agreed.

But today our concept of virginity says it consists in the absence of a sexual act (sex-act virginity) and the non-contact of the male seed with the female egg (seed-act virginity). In this view, Mary would not need a miraculous birthing to retain her virginity. Our impulse is to behold Mary as a real mother giving birth in the normal manner, without any prejudice to her virginity. This comment, however, does not obviate the mystery of virgin birth and in making it I do not intend to do so. The Fathers of the Church hold the greater authority in this matter and I would leave it so.

Saint Ignatius of Antioch (A.D. 35-107), writing during apostolic times, declared that Mary was a virgin and that the birthing of her son "was a mystery which must be proclaimed aloud" (*Ephesians*). Augustine believed in the miracle model and said it witnessed the power of God. "The ground of the mystery is the power of him who permits it to happen" (*Letter*).

Mary remains a virgin. Christian tradition believes that Mary's virginity after the birth is implied in sacred Scripture and flows from the undivided gift of her heart to God alone at the annunciation.

The Gospels seem to imply that Mary had other children.

Luke says that Mary gave birth to her firstborn son (2:7). Would that not mean she had more offspring? No. The expression "firstborn son" was a legal one and did not imply the begetting of other children.

Matthew reports that Joseph had no relations with Mary "until" she bore a son (1:25). But, in the original language, this way of speaking makes no judgment about the future. We would not use the phrase this way, but Matthew did.

The Gospels speak of the "brothers and sisters" of Jesus in several instances. For example, "Is this not the carpenter, the son of Mary and the brother of James and Joses and

Judas and Simon, and are not his sisters here with us?" (Mark 6:3).

But their absence in the narrative of the Finding in the Temple seems to indicate that there were no other children. And since Jesus entrusted the care of Mary to John at Calvary, it may be concluded that if she had other sons, Jesus would have entrusted her to one of them. Moreover, the historical belief in Mary's perpetual virginity was not contested at a time when the memory of the "brothers and sisters" of Jesus was very much alive.

Popular piety in the Eastern Church used the story from the *Book of James* (see Chapter 3) about Joseph being a widower with children of his own to support this belief. So the "brothers of Jesus" would be Joseph's children, not Mary's. Scholarly opinion in the Western Church, led by Saint Jerome, concluded that the word *brothers* in the original could have meant cousins as well as actual brothers.

Not until the fourth century was there any major denial of Mary's perpetual virginity. A man named Helvidius had shocked his contemporaries with his contention that Mary had other children. Saint Jerome wrote a book—*Against Helvidius*—in which he presented a robust rebuttal:

> [B]ecause my brothers have become seriously disturbed and scandalized by his [Helvidius's] ravings, the axe of the Gospel must now be laid at the roots of the barren tree and the tree must be delivered to the flames with its unfruitful leaves, so that he who has never learned to speak might learn at length to hold his tongue.
> —*Saint Jerome,* Against Helvidius

Jerome wrote this book in A.D. 383. He is the first Latin writer to compose a work devoted to Mariology—a theological study of Mary.

Nine years later, Bishop Bonosus in southern Italy mounted another challenge to Mary's perpetual virginity, again claiming she had other children. Arianism was still a force in Christianity and Bonosus was affected by it. In A.D.

392, Pope Siricius convened a regional Council at Capua to deal with Bonosus. Saint Ambrose defended the Church's traditional teaching on the issue. He left the mark of his prudent and forceful personality on the Council. In 1992, Pope John Paul II went to Capua to celebrate the sixteen-hundredth anniversary of the ancient Council and so re-confirm its teachings about Mary's perpetual virginity and its relation to the Incarnation. He delivered an address on the theme that studying Mary helps us to know who Jesus is.

Helvidius and Bonosus have found companionable disciples in our own day. Both fundamentalists and most scholarly Protestants believe Mary had other children. According to a report in the *Los Angeles Times*, some Catholic biblical scholars have re-opened the question of whether Jesus had real brothers and sisters.

Within the rules of modern historical method, Father John Meier concludes "the most probable opinion is that the brothers and sisters of Jesus were true siblings." Catholic scholar Pheme Perkins of Boston College contends that calling Jesus' brothers cousins is "plain ridiculous." But she does not rule out the possibility that "the references to Jesus' brothers and sisters could have meant 'step-siblings'—Joseph's children by a previous marriage."

Father Joseph Fitzmyer offers a more sober scholarly evaluation:

> One cannot solve easily, on the basis of New Testament evidence alone the question whether Jesus' brothers and sisters have to be understood in the strict sense of siblings or in the broad sense of kinsmen, relatives. The latter possibility is certainly not ruled out.
> —*Joseph Fitzmyer, S.J.*, A Christological Catechism

In evaluating present discussions, I believe we should recall that the faith of the Church (East and West) both in its theology and liturgy has long held the doctrine that Mary was "ever a virgin." The historical-critical method has not disproved this and by its own rules says that its conclusions are only probable, not certain. Beyond this the Church asks us to uphold the "principle of totality," meaning that we must look at the whole picture which includes Apostolic tradition, Scripture, liturgical practice, ecumenical councils and the magisterium.

Interestingly, there has never been a need for the direct use of the teaching authority of the Church to reinforce these teachings about Mary's perpetual virginity since there has been a massive unanimity in Church history about it.

In other words, no ecumenical council nor solemn use of papal authority has been needed to affirm it since it has always been believed by the Church and attested to in her liturgy.

Vatican II refers to Mary over thirty times as Virgin, Virgin Mother, Ever Virgin. Our creeds speak of Jesus as being "born of the Virgin Mary." Our liturgy refers to Mary as "Ever Virgin Mother of Jesus Christ, our Lord and God" (*Eucharistic Prayer One*).

The founding fathers of Protestantism—Luther, Calvin and Zwingli—and a major Protestant theologian of the twentieth century, Karl Barth, defended Mary's virginal conception of Jesus. But recently a number of Protestant writers and some Catholic ones either deny it or claim it is an open question.

Some argue that the virgin birth does not refer to an actual biological truth but rather to a moral or spiritual one. But the Church has always understood virginal conception and birth to be a biological event, though of course it can have moral and spiritual meanings as well. Which brings us now to our next consideration—the connection between Mary's virginity and our lives.

The Meaning of Mary's Virginity for Us

Mary's virginity is not a devaluation of sexuality. It is common enough to uphold Mary's virginity as an inspiration for us to be pure. The Church Fathers did this in Late Antiquity when faced with the collapse of sexual discipline. In our own culture of sexual permissiveness, we could scarcely be blamed for citing the purity of Mary as a motive for living up to the ideals of sexual restraint.

If the culture tells us that no one can—or need—live out the moral demands related to sex, we would be irresponsible if we did not counter this with examples of chastity. The culture says, "Everybody's doing it." We beg to differ. "Not true. People have lived chaste lives in every period of history, including our own." The example of faithful people today is an essential witness. Mary's virginity is a powerful witness for all seasons of history.

Having said this, we must not conclude that somehow there is something fundamentally wrong with sexuality. Mary's virginity is not a reproach to the act of sex. Her virginity is a positive appeal for respect for the body, not a negative judgment that says the body is somehow bad and that sex is basically an unworthy human act. In fact Mary's virginity is a celebration of the sacredness of the body. Mary did not shed her body in her virginity. She did not become an angel.

The message of her virginity for married people is the same. Have a reverence for each other's bodies. Treat the bodily act of sex as a holy act that participates in God's creativity and love. There is no doubt that this message has been clouded from time to time in Church history. Christians have been influenced by periodic bouts of hostility to the flesh. The Manicheans in early Christianity said the flesh was evil. Some Christians believed this and unhappily used virginity as a weapon against the flesh.

In the Middle Ages, the Cathari and the Albigensians resurrected the idea of the intrinsic evil of the body—again having an unwholesome influence on some Catholics. We all know that Puritanism and Victorianism communicated a suspicion of the body and sex and encumbered sexuality with undue guilt and repression. Catholics were not immune to these movements as was evident in the oppressive impact of Jansenism.

This woeful history of hostility to the body and sex has taken its toll in misuse of the role of Mary's virginity in our religious vision. It has also been employed to demote women to inferior status, a point made by some feminist critiques of Marian devotion. But the abuse does not take away the use. In other words, just because Mary's virginity has been misinterpreted in the past does not mean there is no correct understanding of her role.

Mary's virginity is a call to honor the correct use of sex and affirm the sacredness of the body. Mary honored her body by giving it totally to the Holy Spirit. The Son of God took his blood and bone from Mary. Her message to married people is no less the same. For should not couples rejoice in the holiness of their bodies and the sacred mystery of their sexual bond?

It is just as evident that Mary's virginity appeals to singles who seek life's highest ideals as well as to monks, nuns and priests. They, too, must treasure the sanctity of their bodies while they appreciate that sexuality is a holy act that may only be exercised in marriage.

Further, who can doubt that Mary's virginity could and should be a precious gift to our society where the moral compass has been swayed by the winds of sexual self-indulgence and a narcissistic vision of the flesh which has caused so much family breakdown, personal despair and psychological pain?

Flowing from this is the fidelity that attaches itself to both virginity and marriage. Mary vowed herself absolutely to God. Husbands and wives vow themselves absolutely to each other in union with God. Fidelity is demanded of all. Does not the fidelity of Mary inspire couples? Does not the fidelity of couples encourage and inspire those today who live as dedicated singles or embrace the consecrated life in celibacy and virginity?

The Virgin Mary is a friend to God's gift of our bodies and their role in our personal development. After all, not only did God give her a body, she gave one to him as well.

Nor would she look fretfully at sex. Her first great act of intercession occurred at a wedding. By God's will her virginity helps all of us appreciate the sanctity of the body and sexuality. For this, let us praise the Lord.

The doctrinal heart of Mary's virginity is the truth that her child was the Son of God. It is sometimes easy to forget that Mary's virginity is more than a stoic act of sexual renunciation taken by a determined young Jewish woman. This view is caused by our tendency to project ourselves into others' lives. If we thought of renouncing sex it would be most likely a calculated act, weighing the alternatives, evaluating the pros and cons, the effect on our health, our psychological states and our reputation in the neighborhood. It might be motivated by disgust with the tawdriness of the culture, a nostalgia for the simple life, a drive to get away from people, from the tensions of the world.

What I am driving at is that I sense most of us take a very pragmatic view of sexual renunciation, if indeed we ever think of it at all. We can scarcely see it in any other terms than a pragmatic decision based on rational and emotional terms. I do not doubt that there are people who view celibacy or virginity as calls from God. Such calls and responses clearly occur in our day. I teach at Pope John XXIII seminary and see fresh examples of this every year as the new class arrives.

When examining the virginity of Mary we need to accept the utter uniqueness of what happened to her. I hope it is obvious to you that she was not making a mere pragmatic decision. The annunciation was far more than a purely rational matter. Mary's virginity must be seen always in the context of revelation and faith.

We have no way of knowing whether she made a vow of virginity prior to the annunciation. One writer says that, because of her preservation from original sin, she had a "virginal inclination." Even if true, that must be measured against the fact she planned to marry Joseph. Some writers believe that Mary and Joseph made a pact to live a sex-free marriage, a conclusion that remains speculative in my judgment. The revelation at the annunciation made the difference in the outcome of their marriage.

The revelatory event of the annunciation changed Mary's life. Mary is faced with an angel of God making her the most breathtaking proposal in history. Here we have divine mystery in its most loving form. This is not a case of a nervous bridegroom proposing to a fine young maiden. This is God speaking to the freedom of a young Jewish woman in a quiet hamlet far from the noise of the great cities of the world.

This is a religious experience that can only be remotely imagined by us, an I-Thou encounter qualitatively unique, even by the standards of other biblical meetings such as those of Abraham, Moses and Isaiah with the Lord God.

Why? Because the intimacy proposed is so remarkable and unexpected. Because the Son of God asks for a home in her womb. Because the Spirit of God will cause the conception to take place. Because her child will be like no other that could be born—fully human indeed, but also the Son of the living God.

We have become so accustomed to the story that our spiritual cataracts understandably cloud over the uniqueness and originality of the event. We need to look at the scene again with fresh eyes and with faith heightened and attuned to the most singular encounter between a woman and God which has ever happened.

No other woman has received such a request. No other woman has conceived such as child. Once God's Son was housed in Mary's womb, all the other faith truths we affirm about her fall in place. The ten images we discuss in this book flow from the single truth that her child was the Son of God. We sing at Christmas, "O come, let us adore him, Christ the Lord." We love all the babies of the world. We adore only one of them.

All accounts of mystical experiences from the testimony of the saints are helpful to us here because they give us some sense of the texture of the encounter at Nazareth removed in time, yet ever present to us, especially at liturgy and when we say the joyful mysteries of the rosary.

The annunciation is a "peak event" which determined Mary's virginity, not just in birthing Jesus, but because having given birth to Christ, Mary has a child to whom no other could compare. In her Son, Mary generates the New Creation itself. Here is a fulfillment any mother would dream of, but could not have imagined until it actually happened. When God is your child, you have arrived at an unequaled completeness.

Mary's virginity is a way to showing us how to have a total and undivided heart for God. It is easy to think of virginity in terms of abstinence from sex. That is true, but inadequate. The purpose of abstaining from sex is to give one's heart totally to God. It is a matter of love. The Virgin Mary gave her heart to God alone. At the annunciation she made a renunciation, not just of sexuality, but also of her will and heart. Her *fiat*—a great yes to God—initiated a process of sacrificial love that would deepen for the rest of her life. She embarked on the pilgrimage of faith we discussed in Chapter Two.

God asked her to practice selfless love. She said yes. Her virginal consecration expressed that selfless love in a concrete manner. When you think about it, what else counts in life more than selfless love? Saint Paul wrote about love in 1 Corinthians 13, noting that nothing else matters but love. No virtue, no achievement, not even giving all your money to the poor or martyrdom means anything if it is not done with love.

Mary excelled at such love of God and others. In the mystery of her love for her child she had a privilege no other mother has known. Here was the Son of God himself in her very home. I will not venture to imagine the state of her awareness of her son's divinity. I can confidently say that if we asked her how she loved her son, I know she would tell us, "I loved my Jesus with all my mind, I loved him with all my strength, I loved him with all my heart."

I believe her gift of virginity began with the Holy Spirit's conception of Jesus and continued for the rest of her life because she was granted the gift of the undivided heart. This was the faith intuition of the early Church and its insight has possessed the hearts of Catholic believers ever since. Mary's ability to love God and others so totally, with a sense of the unity of love, should have great inspirational value for us since her humanity is so like ours. Here is a woman for all seasons and homes and neighborhoods. With God's help we can all love as she did. With God's grace may it happen to us.

Her virginity is a path to availability for the needs of people begun during the nine days of prayer that preceded Pentecost. There is a tendency to treat virginity as a separation of the person from the needs of everyday life. Mary is a good example of availability, not separation. First, she was a mother and keeper of the family home. She raised a child and did what was necessary for the maintenance of their home at Nazareth. At Cana, she became involved in a problem at a wedding. At Calvary, she stood bravely by her Son. At Pentecost, she was right in the middle of the community, praying with them for the coming of the Spirit.

Mary's virginity did not isolate her from the physical, spiritual and emotional needs of others. Since her Assumption into heaven, Mary has become available to the whole Church. So involved is she now with our needs, that we entreat her as "Mother of the Church."

Just as her Son was the Man for Others, so Mary is the Woman for Others. Her virginal availability is a model for every believer whether married, single or a member of the consecrated life. No state of life should be an excuse to run away from life. No life-style ought to be a refuge from the world's needs. Love is only love when it is exercised toward a real God and real people.

Cloister walls do not necessarily isolate the nuns from the needs of the world. In fact I have been the beneficiary of the prayers and concern of the Sioux City Iowa Carmel for the forty-four years of my priesthood. I have felt their impact and known their effectiveness.

I have seen firsthand their influence on the local city. From their posts at prayer they radiated faith, hope and love and service to thousands of others, even though they remain within their virginal cloister. Their walls are really windows into the infinite which turns their eyes outward to the world and its need for prayer, love and salvation. They retain their capacity to become saints, not just in their newest one—Edith Stein, Sister Teresa Benedicta—but also in the countless members worldwide who have been living the Carmelite ideal for so many centuries.

Prayer

In this reflection, I want to share with you a litany composed by the members of the Pax Christi movement. It has a contemporary ring to it that I hope you will find a source of prayer.

Litany of Mary of Nazareth

Glory to you, God our Creator...
Breathe into us new life, new meaning.
Glory to you, God our Savior...
Lead us in the way of peace and justice.
Glory to you, healing Spirit...
Transform us to empower others.

Mary, wellspring of peace...*Be our guide.*
Model of strength
Model of gentleness
Model of trust
Model of courage
Model of patience
Model of openness
Model of perseverance

Mother of the liberator...*Pray for us.*

Mother of the homeless
Mother of the dying
Mother of the nonviolent
Widowed mother
Mother of a political prisoner
Mother of the condemned
Mother of the executed criminal
. . .

Comforter of the afflicted...*Lead us to life.*
Cause of our joy
Political refugee
Seeker of sanctuary
First disciple
Sharer in Christ's passion
Seeker of God's will
Witness to Christ's resurrection
. . .

Closing Prayer

Mary, Queen of Peace,
We entrust our lives to you.
Shelter us from war, hatred and oppression.
Teach us
to live in peace,
to educate ourselves for peace.
Inspire us to act justly,
to revere all that God has made.
Root peace firmly in our hearts
and in our world.
Amen.
     —*Pax Christi U.S.A.*

IMMACULATE CONCEPTION
Statue at grotto, Lourdes, France

CHAPTER SIX

❖

Immaculate Conception

O Mother, how pure you are.

You are untouched by sin.

Yours was the privilege

to carry God within you.

—*Liturgy of the Hours*

I Saw a Lady

I had gone down one day with two other girls to a bank of the river Gave when suddenly I heard a kind of rustling sound. I turned my head toward the field by the side of the river but the trees seemed quite still and the noise was evidently not from them. Then I looked up and caught sight of the cave where I saw a lady wearing a lovely white dress with a bright belt. On top of each of her feet was a pale yellow rose, the same color as her rosary beads.

At this I rubbed my eyes, thinking I was seeing things, and I put my hands into the fold of my dress where my rosary was. I wanted to make the sign of the cross, but for the life of me I just couldn't manage it and my hands just fell down. Then the lady made the sign of the cross herself and at the second attempt I managed to do the same, though my hands were trembling. Then I began to say the rosary while the lady let the beads slip through her fingers, without moving her lips. When I stopped saying the Hail Mary, she immediately vanished.

I asked my two companions if they had noticed anything, but they said no.... I came back next Sunday, feeling myself drawn to the place.... I went back each day for fifteen days and each time, except one Monday and one Friday, the lady appeared and told me to look for a stream and wash in it and to see that the priests built a chapel there. I must also pray, she said, for the conversion of sinners. I asked her many times what she meant by that, but she only smiled. Finally, with outstretched arms and eyes looking up to heaven, she told me she was the Immaculate Conception.

> —From a letter of Saint Bernadette about her vision of
> Mary at Lourdes, Liturgy of the Hours

I was in high school when the film, *The Song of Bernadette* came out. Jennifer Jones played the part of Bernadette and won an Academy Award for her innocent and unaffected portrayal of the peasant teenager who had a vision of Mary.

The film was a miracle in itself, honestly reporting a profound religious experience and honoring the premise of a vision and subsequent miracles. In cinematic terms alone it was one of those productions where the actors formed an ensemble, none upstaging the other, all seamlessly melded into a harmonious creation.

I remember the first time I saw it and how deeply it affected me. On my way out of the theater I was surprised to overhear a patron say to her companion, "It was a lovely film. Of course I don't believe a word of it." I understood better then the inscription of the film that addressed the faith issue at hand:

> To those who believe, no explanation is necessary.
> To those who do not, no explanation is possible.

That was probably one of my first theology lessons. Without faith the supernatural is an unending puzzle. But with faith a whole world of meaning opens up. My family and my Church had passed on the faith to me. I was familiar with the grotto scene at Lourdes from seeing it hundreds of times at my parish church. *The Song of Bernadette* opened up its story in ways I had never imagined. Over the years I have seen it many times and renewed my experience of the mystery of Mary as the Immaculate Conception.

I recall that there was a debate in those days as to whether Mary should be visibly portrayed by an actress, as the film actually did, with Linda Darnell taking the part. Some argued that the niche in the grotto should just be filled with light since the supernatural can never be adequately presented in human terms.

This reflects the old debate about how seriously we should take the Incarnation. You may recall that the first heresy in Christianity claimed that the Son of God never really took on a body. Those people resisted the possibility of such a "demotion" of God. Christianity rejected that teaching and stated that Jesus was born of the flesh and blood of Mary and that he was truly human and died a true death on the cross.

It is a very Catholic trait to want visible representations of Jesus and Mary and the saints. We have never accepted iconoclasm, a view that our churches should have no statues or icons. We are a sacramental church, meaning not just that we use bread, wine, oil and water as necessary, effective signs of grace, but also that we are comfortable with the visible reminders of the heavenly kingdom and its citizens. In those far-off days of my adolescence I sided with those who made Mary physically present in the film. I still do.

I think it remains an issue because the doctrine of the Immaculate Conception confronts us with blunt biological imagery as well as a transcendent religious mystery. We are made to think about processes of conception, the origin of life in the womb and the development of the unborn child.

I should dispel at the outset a common misunderstanding of the mystery. I am not talking about the virginal conception and birth of Jesus. Some think that the Immaculate Conception refers to the virginal conception of Jesus by the power of the Holy Spirit. In their minds, because there was no human father or human sexual act, the conception of Jesus was "clean" or immaculate.

The term *immaculate* comes from the Latin, meaning without stain. Those who mistake virgin birth for immaculate conception argue from a negative view of conception as though it implies a stain, that there is something slightly bad about the sexual act that leads to conception.

Unfortunately, this is a very old idea. Some Church Fathers believed this. When Augustine concluded that original sin is communicated through the act of carnal generation he cast a negative view of the sexual act. He was probably also still influenced by his days with Manichaeism, a pagan sect that looked unfavorably on the flesh and sex as fundamentally evil.

What is pertinent here is the rejection of the false idea of the Immaculate Conception. The teaching refers to the conception of Mary and her freedom from original sin. It is not a comment on the act of carnal generation, but rather a belief about the powerful love of God and the divine plan that Mary would be the mother of the savior, the Son of God. As I have insisted before, the role of Mary must always be seen in the light of her relation to Christ.

This little story may help. A Catholic boy was telling an older man—a university professor—about the greatness of Mary, the mother of Jesus. The professor smiled at the boy's enthusiasm and tried to disarm him by saying, "But there is no difference between her and my mother." The confident boy replied, "You may think so, but let me tell you there is an enormous difference between the sons."

We need to see Mary in the broad horizon of God's plan to save the world from sin and give people divine life and the possibility of eternal happiness in heaven. None of us could choose our mothers, but if we could we would naturally select the greatest woman imaginable. The Son of God was able to pick his mother and endow her with the greatest of graces, freedom from original sin. We should not be amazed that the Son of God could imagine beforehand what kind of a mother he would want.

When James Whistler painted a picture of his mother, did he not have on his mind what she would be like before he ever assembled his colors? When complimented on this portrait, he said, "Well you know how it is. One tries to make one's mother as nice as he can."

The Development of the Teaching

The Bible says that Jeremiah and John the Baptist were sanctified in the womb. This implies there was a need to be made holy. Jeremiah and John were sanctified after they were conceived. Mary was sanctified from the moment she was conceived. The New Testament provides hints of this truth, though it will take centuries of faith and prayer to unfold it.

Luke's Gospel reports that Gabriel addressed Mary as "full of grace" or more accurately, "highly favored one."

Elizabeth declared that Mary was "most blessed among
women." In her Magnificat, Mary says of herself that "All
nations will call me blessed." These words refer to the adult
Mary and, as yet, do not obviously imply that she was immaculately conceived or somehow sanctified in the womb.
This was a teaching that evolved in the reflection of theologians, the liturgy of the Church and the devotion of the
people.

We have already seen some of the early building blocks
of the theology about Mary, each of which was always related to a truth about the Lord Jesus. Justin called her the
New Eve whose obedience contrasted with the disobedience of the first Eve. Irenaeus preached that Mary's obedience untied the knot created by Eve's disobedience.

By the fourth century, Ephrem was prepared to extol
the holiness of Mary, lifting it into a new realm:

> You Jesus and your mother alone
> are beautiful in every way.
> In you no stain,
> in your mother no spot.

The liturgies of the East—then and now—call Mary "All
Holy."

In the fifth century, the theological question arose in the
Western Church about whether Mary had original sin. The
question emerged from the debate caused by Pelagius who
argued that people can become holy by personal effort
"aided by grace." But his idea of grace was external, meaning only the example of Jesus and the inspirational encour-
agement of Scripture and other sources of moral motivation.

So Pelagius really teaches that we save ourselves by our
willpower. People asked him how the doctrine of Baptism
fit into his theory. He replied that Baptism liberated the
human will to practice perfect obedience to God. He had an
optimistic view of human nature and its potential. He
failed to recognize sufficiently the enduring moral weaknesses that exist after Baptism. He had a superficial under-

standing of grace.

His ideas had a strong appeal to the educated upper classes influenced by the philosophy of Stoicism. Bright, confident aristocrats, sick of the corruption of Late Antiquity, formed coteries of strivers after perfection. Pelagius was their guru and inspiration.

He was creating sanctimonious cliques in the upper reaches of Christian society. These self-willed ascetics really saw no need for any divine help other than its inspiration seen in the life of Jesus. They were not babies, clinging to the divine bosom in humble dependence on God. They were strong-willed adults creating their own salvation.

The smug superiority of these "perfect" Catholics had no appeal for Saint Augustine. Their behavior and the teachings of Pelagius, their mentor, prompted Augustine to probe the relationship between nature and grace and produce a masterpiece of insight into it. Unlike Pelagius, Augustine was fascinated by babies. The extent of their helplessness made him think of his weakness before God. He likened his relationship to God to that of a baby at his mother's breast, utterly dependent on her as the only source of life.

> [W]hat am I but a creature suckled on your milk and feeding on yourself, the food that never perishes? And what is any man, if he is only a man? Let the strong and mighty laugh at men like me: let us, the weak and the poor, confess our sins to you.
> —*Augustine*, Confessions

Augustine disagreed with Pelagius's idea that we can save ourselves by developing a strong will. Augustine saw Baptism as more than a liberation of the will to obey God absolutely. Baptism was also a liberation from a primal sin, whose effects still endured after Baptism. It was Augustine who named the fatal act of our first parents, "original sin."

Due to the sin of Adam and Eve, we have lost original holiness and are born deprived of grace. We need grace to be born again and to sustain us through the challenges of life. Grace, therefore, is more than the good example of others or a spiritual pep talk from the Bible, valuable though that is.

Grace is an interior work of the Holy Spirit, transforming us into friends of God and accompanying us through a lifelong process of healing. Baptism delivers us from original sin, but we need further graces to walk through a lifetime of being healed from the power of sin.

In pondering the question of how we inherit original sin, Augustine judged that it occurred in carnal generation. Hence, at conception we enter life deprived of grace and bereft of original justification.

Once Augustine had laid out his teachings on original sin and grace, and the way in which original sin was transmitted, it was inevitable that people would wonder how this applied to Mary. Was she conceived and born in original sin? If so, how can we call her, "All Holy Mary?" Moreover, as a creature, did not Mary need salvation just like everyone else? Augustine heard these questions and made a great exception in her case.

> We must make an exception of the holy virgin Mary, concerning whom I wish to raise no question when it touches the subject of sins, out of honor to the Lord. For from him we know what abundance of grace for overcoming sin in every particular...was conferred upon her who had the merit to conceive and bear him who undoubtedly had no sin.
> —*Augustine*, Nature and Grace

Augustine did not explain this great exception. He left that to the doctrinal development which took place in the next fourteen centuries in the Western Church.

While theologians would wonder and argue about Mary's conception and birth, the liturgical feasts of Mary forged ahead.

✳ *A feast of Mary's nativity was celebrated in the East in the late sixth century. Normally, a saint's feast commemorated the saint's death and "birthday" into heaven. But here was a liturgy remembering her earthly birthday.*

✳ *In the West a feast of the conception of Mary appeared in England in the year 1060. After the Norman Conquest (1066), this feast expanded to the continent and was known as the Immaculate Conception.*

✳ *In 1695 Innocent XII approved a Mass of the Immaculate Conception for the whole Church.*

✳ *In 1708 Clement XI made it a holy day of obligation.*

Despite these feasts, theologians were slower to accept the Immaculate Conception. When the Canons of Lyons established this liturgy in their diocese, they received a surprising and stinging rebuke from none other than the greatest troubadour and defender of Mary in the Middle Ages, Saint Bernard of Clairvaux. His famous letter to the Canons stated:

> If it is appropriate to say what the Church believes and if what she believes is true, then I say that the glorious (Virgin) conceived by the Holy Spirit, but was not also herself conceived in this way. I say that she gave birth as a virgin, but not that she was born of a virgin. For otherwise what would be the prerogative of the Mother of God?

Bernard was saying that in order to be conceived and born without original sin, Mary would have to have been conceived like Jesus by the Holy Spirit. She would also need to have been born of a virgin as Jesus. This is the only way she could be exempted from original sin. But this was manifestly not the case, so she was conceived in original sin. Hence the Immaculate Conception could not be a teaching of the Church. However, Bernard deferred to Rome as the final arbiter in this issue.

I should report here two of the questions and answers given by medieval theologians: (1)Was Mary free of all actual sins? Yes. (2)Did Mary need redemption by the saving work of Christ? Yes.

Saint Thomas Aquinas himself could not see how Mary could be immaculately conceived. If this had happened she would not need redemption. But as a creature she did need to be saved. Indeed he believed she was sanctified in the womb and never committed any actual sins. That is why her liturgical feast of her earthly birth was legitimate. Because she was free of actual sins we could call her All Holy. The bone of contention for Aquinas was Mary's need for redemption.

His position is a bit confusing for us because he envisioned two steps in the emergence of Mary: first, conception by carnal generation; second, the animation of her body, meaning the gift of her soul with reason and will. Her conception would have made her like all humans and thus an inheritor of original sin.

Once she receives a soul she could then be sanctified from the stain of original sin. Aquinas believed that only Christ was conceived without original sin and this was the beginning and origin of his salvation work. Aquinas believed Mary was sanctified in the womb much the same as Jeremiah and the Baptist.

> God did not so limit his law to the power of the
> sacraments, but that He can bestow His grace, by
> special privilege on some before they are born from the
> womb....Original sin is transmitted through the origin
> [meaning conception] inasmuch as through the origin
> the human nature is transmitted, and original sin,
> properly speaking, affects the nature. And this takes
> place when the offspring conceived is animated.
> Wherefore nothing hinders the offspring conceived
> from being sanctified after animation.
> —*Aquinas*, Summa

In the mind of Aquinas, if Mary were conceived without original sin she would not need redemption. But Mary was a creature and did need it. So how can the dilemma be solved? It took the genius of Duns Scotus (1265-1308) to resolve the problem. He made two important contributions. First he said that preservative salvation was greater than medicinal redemption. To be preserved from original sin was a greater grace than to be set free from it. Second, he composed an explanation to show how Mary was preserved from original sin.

We say today that preventive medicine is more desirable than curative medicine since it protects us from the disease in the first place. At Mass we pray for forgiveness of sins in the penitential rite. Then we go on to beg the Father for the preventive graces we need so we will not fall into sin again.

Scotus worked from this formula: Whatever was possible and eminently fitting for God to do, that he did. God could do it. It was fitting that he do so. He did it. Scotus said it was possible for God to preserve Mary from original sin. Jesus, her Son, was the most perfect redeemer. He had the greatest ability to apply redemption to one creature, certainly to his mother.

The most perfect form of this salvation would be to preserve Mary from original sin rather than rescue her from it after conception. Preserving grace does not do away with original sin. But it does prevent it. Mary needed Jesus as redeemer to preserve her from original sin. Some refer to this teaching of Scotus as the theology of abundance. It probes beyond what seem to be the boundaries of divine love and generosity and discovers new horizons. It climbs the upper reaches of divine love rather than more restrictive views. Scotus did not settle the matter for theologians, but he gave a brilliant alternative that ultimately prevailed in 1854.

I Am the Immaculate Conception

On July 18, 1830, Catherine Laboure, a young member of the Sisters of Charity of Saint Vincent de Paul was abruptly awakened from her sleep at 11:30 P.M. A shining child appeared to her and led her to the chapel. The Blessed Mother appeared to her and talked with her for two hours. On November 27, she had a second vision. Mary appeared standing on a globe with shafts of light streaming from her hands toward earth.

Surrounding the scene were the words, "O Mary, conceived without sin, pray for us who have recourse to you." This was like a picture which was then reversed. On the other side, Catherine saw the letter *M* with a cross above it with two hearts, one crowned with thorns and the other with a sword going through it. Twelve stars framed this side of the medal, echoing the vision of the Woman clothed with the sun and crowned with twelve stars in the Book of Revelation, Chapter 12.

Catherine heard a voice telling her to have a medal struck representing what she saw in the vision. The voice said that all who wore the medal would receive great graces through the intercession of the Mother of God. Catherine received several more visions of a similar kind until September 1831. In June 1832, the first fifteen hundred medals were produced.

The archbishop of Paris gave approval of the visions and the use of the medal in 1836, even though Catherine resolutely refused to appear for an interview. She bound Father Amadel, her confessor and promoter of the medal and its devotion, to secrecy regarding her identity. Catherine lived in obscurity in a rural convent for the rest of her life. Not until eight months before her death in 1876 did she finally reveal her identity. Her funeral was an occasion of an outburst of popular veneration for her. The Church canonized her in 1947.

Catherine's vision occurred about twenty years before Pius IX made the doctrine of the Immaculate Conception a dogma of the Church. The enormous popularity of the Miraculous Medal, as it came to be called, and its prayer to Mary "conceived without sin," planted the doctrine in millions of devout hearts who wore the medal faithfully about their necks.

Popular devotion had reinforced what centuries of theological discussion and royal pressures had failed to do. For example, in the two centuries between 1600 and 1800, the Jesuits published three hundred works on the Immaculate Conception. European princes supported the doctrine and the king of Spain sent several delegations to the Vatican to ask for a definition. Then came the Enlightenment which threw a cold wash over Catholic devotion for a time. Yet in the very land where the French Revolution took place, Mary appeared to Catherine Laboure and requested the devotion of the Miraculous Medal, a devotion which swept the Catholic world.

The Making of a Dogma

At the beginning of his pontificate, Pius IX received an increasing number of requests for a definition of the doctrine. In 1847 he was impressed by a book by Giovanni Perrone on the Immaculate Conception: *Can It Be Defined by Dogmatic Decree?* It moved the pope to establish a commission of cardinals and theologians to advise him. This led to a meeting of cardinals to whom he addressed two questions. Should he define the privilege? How should he do it?

The cardinals said he should define it. They counseled him to ask the opinion of the world's bishops. For this purpose he wrote an encyclical, *Ubi Primum,* and sent it to the bishops in 1849. Of 603 bishops consulted, 543 favored definition. Four opposed the idea and the rest abstained. From 1850 to 1854 the pope supervised seven drafts of a proposed document for the definition. Five of these drafts were worked on by a commission of 21 cardinals and a large number of theologians.

After a number of last-minute amendments the bull,

Ineffabilis Deus, was promulgated on December 8, 1854. The definition itself reads as follows:

> We declare, pronounce and define that the doctrine
> which holds that the most Blessed Virgin Mary, in the
> first instant of her conception, by a singular grace and
> privilege granted by Almighty God, in view of the
> merits of Jesus Christ, the savior of the human race, was
> preserved free from all stain of original sin, is a doctrine
> revealed by God and therefore to be believed firmly and
> constantly by all the faithful.

Four years later, as if to confirm the dogma, Mary appeared to Bernadette Soubirous in the grotto at Lourdes. After persistent requests from Bernadette as to her name, Mary said, "I am the Immaculate Conception." This vision and private revelation was to have even greater influence than the one Sister Catherine received. Over five million pilgrims visit Lourdes every year singing *aves* to Mary Immaculate. A few receive physical cures. The number who receive spiritual healing is beyond counting.

Reflection

Mary needed to be liberated from original sin. Christ used preserving grace so she never inherited this state. We also need salvation from original sin. For us Christ, through the Church, uses rescuing grace in the sacrament of Baptism. One value of the doctrine of Mary's Immaculate Conception is that it draws us to meditate on the impact of original sin in our lives.

Why is the doctrine of original sin of enduring importance for us? Because it is the best way of answering the question, "What do you think of human nature?" Considering all the debates about human nature, I have boiled down three major versions for my own use.

The great Protestant reformer John Calvin took a grim view of human nature—basically claiming it intrinsically bad. Christ's redemption saves us but we remain intractably prone to evil.

The sunny and popular French philosopher, Jean Jacques Rousseau, had a starry-eyed vision of human nature. He declared it is intrinsically good. He says we have no original sin to worry about. Christ's redemption is unnecessary.

The ever-practical bishop and pastor, Augustine of Hippo, taught that human nature is good but flawed. Augustine, who coined the term original sin, was all too aware of the possible depths of evil of which people were capable. He attributed that to original sin, which is a state in which we are deprived of grace and original holiness. But he knew that with Baptism we are delivered from the guilt that accompanied that state, while we still retain the weaknesses and tendencies to evil which that condition begets.

But God's grace in the sacraments and other sources available to us helps us to undergo a lifelong process of healing the effects of sin and brings us to the desired personal integration and proper use of our freedom.

We are like Mary in that we have been freed from original sin. Because of her becoming Mother of God she has been granted a capacity to love God and others that is exceptional. She knows our needs and prays with us and for us so that our healing process will never cease. We can become saints and are called to holiness. In a certain sense, a saint is a sinner making progress in holiness.

Here are some reflective questions to consider on this issue:

✳ *What is my vision of human nature?*

✳ *When I see how awful people can be, such as in the Holocaust, in the Oklahoma City bombing, or in teenagers killing their newborn infants, what do I think is the real cause of such evil?*

✱ *How do I balance my perceptions of the mix of good and evil in human beings?*

✱ *How has the Holy Spirit's grace-filled action been present in my life?*

We, Too, Are Holy Temples of God

Mary does not differ from us because she possessed these gifts [of grace]. It is her possession of them from the beginning, and incomparably, that is the sole difference between her and us. As for the content of this gift, its nature and intrinsic meaning, the eternal Father could not intend anything for the mother of his incarnate Son, without intending it for us too, and giving it to us in the sacrament of justification.

For us too he eternally intended this saving grace from the beginning, in his eternity, even though it was only effected in us after the beginning of our earthly, temporal life, in order that it might be plain that it is all his grace, that nothing in our salvation belongs to us of ourselves.

God has eternally kept his eternal love in readiness for us too, so that in the moment we call our baptism, he may come into the depths of our heart. For we too are redeemed, saved, marked with God's indelible seal.

We too have been made the holy temple of God. In us too the triune God dwells. We too are anointed, hallowed, filled with the light and life of God. We too have been sent by him, from the beginning, into our life, that we too may carry the light of faith and the flame of love through this world's darkness, to the place where we belong, in his eternal radiance.

—*Karl Rahner, S.J.*, Mary, Mother of the Lord

✱ *Why do you think Father Rahner stresses our common identity with Mary in the order of grace?*

✱ *If we, like Mary, have received the graces of salvation, though only after our Baptism, what tasks and challenges does this truth about ourselves present to us?*

✳ *What must we do to renew our Baptism in a practical way?*

Prayer

Father,
you prepared the Virgin Mary
to be the worthy mother of your Son.
You let her share beforehand
in the salvation Christ would bring by his death,
and kept her sinless from the first moment of her
   conception.
Help us by her prayers
to live in your presence without sin. Amen.
>   *—Prayer for the Feast of the*
>   *Immaculate Conception*

OUR LADY OF GUADALUPE
Basilica de Guadalupe, Mexico City, Mexico

CHAPTER SEVEN

* * *

Glorious Assumption

What son would not bring his mother

back to life and would not bring her

into paradise after her death if he could?

—*Saint Francis de Sales,*
  Sermon for Assumption

Love Craves Union With the Beloved

Love in its nature is an Ascension in Christ and an
Assumption in Mary. So closely are love and the
Assumption related that a few years ago, while
instructing a Chinese woman, I found that the one truth
in Christianity which was easiest for her to believe was
the Assumption.

She personally knew a saintly soul who lived on a
mat in the woods, whom thousands of people visited to
receive her blessing. One day according to the belief of
all who knew the saint, she was "assumed" into heaven.

The explanation the convert from Confucianism
gave was: "Her love was so great that her body
followed her soul." One thing is certain: The
Assumption is easy to understand if one loves God
deeply, but it is hard to understand if one loves not....

To a world that worships the body, the Church now
says, "There are two bodies in heaven, one the glorified
nature of Jesus, the other the assumed human nature of
Mary. Love is the secret of the Ascension of the one and
of the Assumption of the other, for love craves unity
with the beloved. The Son returns to the Father in the
unity of the divine nature; and Mary returns to Jesus in
the unity of the human nature. Her nuptial flight is the
event to which our whole generation moves.

—*Archbishop Fulton J. Sheen*, The World's First Love

I had mentioned earlier that my birthday falls on the feast
of Our Lady of Guadalupe. Her image reminds me of her
Assumption. Rays of heavenly glory frame her figure. I
have seen her image several times at her shrine in Mexico
City. As in all great Marian shrines I am touched by the
faith of the pilgrims. It is customary for many to approach
her presence on their knees. Some have moved thus, slowly
and painfully, often for miles.

They do not seem to mind. I think of the pain. They
think of Our Lady. I am a so-called comfort-seeking "modern." There is an inclination to categorize these pilgrims as
peasants from a past long gone. That is unfair and arrogant.

To see them and feel their faith is to be rescued from clinical observations. They are people who live in the same world I do and share the same humanity. They are persons with dreams and worries, hopes and fears, joy and sadness. They seek as much as I ever could the favor of Our Lady.

The remarkable new basilica in Mexico City is a triumph of contemporary architecture, warm, welcoming and designed to bring us all close to the altar despite its vastness. Its oval shape makes this possible. The colors are primary, yet muted so that they focus us on Christ and not on color schemes. A moving walkway is set behind and beneath the sanctuary so that pilgrims may get a closer look at the image of Mary, yet not be a distraction to the worshipers in the body of the Church. Despite a river of pilgrims the shrine is quiet and meditative.

Where did the Guadalupe image come from? In 1531 Our Lady appeared to a Native American named Juan Diego. She asked him to go to the local bishop and request that he build a church on the site of her appearance. Naturally the bishop was reluctant to believe Juan. He asked for a sign.

Mary instructed Juan Diego to gather some roses. Though they were out of season, he found some, wrapped them in his cloak and returned to the bishop. When he unfolded the cloak and the roses fell out, both he and the bishop were astounded to see an image of Mary on Juan's cloak looking exactly the way he had described her.

A shrine was built and the miraculous image became an object of veneration. Up to that time the conversion of the Native Americans in Mexico had been scanty and slow. After the vision, the conversions were quick and far-reaching. Part of the appeal of the image was that it portrayed Mary as a Native American.

The other surprising factor was that it presented Mary clothed with the sun, robed in the glory of the mystery of her Assumption. So often it was imagined that her greatest appeal is as the Madonna with her child. Who could not be attracted to a mother and baby? Yet here the miraculous image shows her in heavenly light. It is her Assumption which appealed to millions, first the Indians and then the rest of the world.

Archbishop Sheen connects divine love with the Assumption. Love craves union with the beloved. Our Lady of Guadalupe, though seemingly far off in glory, actually feels intimate and affectionate. Her Assumption was a work of eternal love. That same love brings her close to us. To go to heaven is not to leave us alone. In the Communion of Saints we believe we have a neighborly relationship with those in heaven.

Though a lover and a beloved be separated on earth by an ocean or a continent, the bond of love in the mind and heart can be as close as fire to a burning log. The miracle of love may dissolve all spaces. Physical presence is desirable, but when it is not available, love maintains the union. In Mary's case, love's gravity brought about her total union with her son. Because Jesus loved his mother so much, he desired to grant her the privilege of bodily Assumption as well as spiritual union after her "falling asleep in the Lord."

There is a distinction between Ascension and Assumption. Jesus ascended to heaven by his own power. Mary is assumed into heaven, not by her power, but by the grace of God.

Who Was the Woman Clothed With the Sun?

Around the year A.D. 90, John, the author of the Book of Revelation, was exiled to the penal colony of Patmos, an island not far from what is today mainland Turkey. The Roman government had put him there under house arrest apparently because his Christian witness was objectionable, especially in the light of the new laws requiring emperor worship.

The risen Christ appeared to him in a vision and commissioned him to be a prophet to the Church suffering persecution. The Lord called John to strengthen the Church, give the people hope and provide them with an interpretation of the tribulations which had shaken their faith.

In the twelfth chapter of his book, he reported a vision that seems to have relevance to our discussion. Walking along the beach by the Aegean Sea, John suddenly saw a woman clothed with the sun, crowned with twelve stars, with the moon under her feet. She was pregnant and in labor to bring forth her son. In front of her is a flame-red dragon prepared to seize her son and destroy him.

Who is this woman? Scripture scholars give many different answers. The Church, in the liturgy for the feast of the Assumption, uses this text for the first reading, implying that the woman is Our Lady of the Assumption. The woman is a mother whose child is mortally threatened by evil. Before the dragon can catch him, the child is swiftly taken up into heaven. In this cameo we have a retelling of both the birth and ascension of the child, the messiah.

In John's Gospel, Jesus calls Mary "woman" at Cana and Calvary. If he had spoken to her as mother he would have been talking to her as his parent. But when he addresses her as woman, he is recognizing her theological role in the history of salvation. At Cana she exercised her religious role as intercessor, not just solving a couple's wine problem, but also inviting Jesus to embark on his public ministry of salvation. At Calvary she is called to be the spiritual mother of the Church.

While we cannot be certain that Saint John the Evangelist is the writer of the Book of Revelation, we can be sure that the book is part of Johannine literature, that it is closely related to the thought and school of Saint John's disciples. Hence when we read that the seer John on the beach sees the "woman" we have some foundation in connecting her with the woman Mary of the Gospel. In this context the term *woman* is a code word.

This woman is clothed with the symbols of creation—sun and stars. She stands on the moon, the sign of night. She is robed in light and controls the darkness under her feet. Like Eve who met the serpent, this woman encounters the dragon (a serpent-like creature). Eve-like, the woman wears the cosmic jewels of the creation story. But unlike Eve who bore sinners, the woman bears the Savior, assaulted by evil, but a victor over sin and ascending into heaven.

The woman is already assumed into heaven. Her sign appeared in the sky, a symbol of heaven. The scene portrays a woman assumed into heaven and a child ascended into heaven. For us who look at the vision of John in faith, it does not take too great a leap of the imagination to connect the woman with Mary and the child with Christ.

It has been said often enough that Scripture gives no account of the Assumption of Mary. Yet this scene in the Apocalypse has so many Marian resonances that I am inclined to see it as the way in which divine revelation has chosen to speak to us about this mystery. Why else would the Church choose this passage for the feast of the Assumption?

Did Mary Die?

The Eastern Church has long held the view that Mary died. The feast of the Dormition (falling asleep) of Mary was established by the emperor Maurice on August 15 in the year 600. Falling asleep has the connotation of also waking up. It implied that death would be followed by a waking up in glory. There is a church of the Dormition in Jerusalem near the Garden of Gethsemane. Tradition holds that it is near the site of Mary's tomb, though this has never been found. There is also a tradition that Mary died at Ephesus. We have no way to prove the authenticity of either claim.

Most Church Fathers believe Mary died. Some thought that because of her Immaculate Conception, being preserved from the sin that brought death, Mary would have no reason to die. Further, she committed no actual sins. True, Jesus was also without original sin, but by the divine plan, Jesus needed to enter death in order to conquer both sin and death.

For Mary the same reason did not apply. Those who

hold this position visualize Mary simply disappearing from earth at what would be her death time. The debate as to whether Mary died or not lingers in discussions related to Mary's Assumption. It is an unresolved issue despite the authority of the Fathers and medieval theologians who believe she died. In a recent catechesis about Mary's Assumption, Pope John Paul II sided with those who believe Mary died.

It should be recalled that whether we die or not, our bodies will be changed and transformed for entrance into heaven. Saint Paul was asked, "What will happen to the living when Christ comes again to judge the world? What will happen to those alive at the second coming?" Paul replied that we shall be changed. Our bodies will be transfigured. Just as Christ rose into a glorified body, so we will be transformed.

> Listen, I will tell you a mystery! We will not all die, but we will all be changed, in a moment, in the twinkling of an eye, at the last trumpet. For the trumpet will sound, and the dead will be raised imperishable, and we will be changed. For this perishable body must put on imperishability and this mortal body must put on immortality.
> —1 Corinthians 15:51-53

The point here is that whether we die or not, we still need a changed, immortal body made ready for our life in heaven. Mary's assumed body (whether she died or not) would need this transformation for her life in heaven.

Pope Sergius established the feast of the Dormition in Rome around 650. He decreed a procession for the feast to give it greater solemnity. Adrian I (772-795) changed the name of the feast to the title of Assumption. From then on the West would stress Mary's bodily assumption, while the East focused on her real death, though also having faith in her assumption as well. The liturgical tradition became one of the strongest supports for the eventual definition of this doctrine. However, Pope Pius XII provided a principle for a proper understanding of the liturgy's role. He said that liturgy does not engender the faith but rather springs from it. Liturgy is a distilling of the faith of the people. The prayer of the people becomes the prayer of the Church.

One of the very earliest homilies about this topic survives from the literature of the East from the bishop of Livias on the left bank of the Jordan.

> It was fitting that the most holy body of Mary, God-bearing body, receptacle of God, divinized, incorruptible, illuminated by divine grace and full of glory...should be entrusted to the earth for a little while and raised up to heaven in glory with her soul pleasing to God.
> —*Theoteknos, Bishop of Livias*

Some Who Doubted the Assumption

One of the most curious of the twists and turns in the development of this doctrine occurred in the early Middle Ages. The Abbot of Corbie, Radbertus, around 860, published a letter which he falsely attributed to Saint Jerome. I am not sure whether he was mistaken or deliberately used Jerome as a pseudonym. At any rate his letter denied that Mary was assumed into heaven, though it was otherwise full of praise for her. This letter with its doubt was inserted into the Office of Readings in the liturgy.

Matters were made worse by another monk, Usuard, who in 875 composed a revised martyrology—a calendar of saints containing a few descriptive words about each one. He stated that the doctrine of the Assumption was based on some apocryphal, legendary and untrustworthy accounts that were popular in the early Church. Therefore we had little authoritative evidence for the doctrine. He added the brittle comment that the Church preferred pious ignorance to apocryphal tales.

Since a portion of the martyrology was read every day in the Liturgy of the Hours, thousands of monks, nuns and others would be reading his expressed doubt every year on

August 15. In a strange counterpoint, somebody published a treatise attributed to Augustine which favored the doctrine of the Assumption. Hence we have the odd case of contradictory writings attributed to people who were not the authors: Pseudo-Jerome vs. Pseudo-Augustine.

Pope Saint Pius V purged the doubts of Radbertus/Pseudo-Jerome and the speculation of Usuard from the liturgy in the mid-sixteenth century. It is hard to know how influential these men were in cooling the faith of people about this teaching. It was unlikely they would directly affect the regular parishioner who would not normally be involved in choir liturgies. But the readings might sway some priests and monks who would be available for preaching the doctrine.

The celebration of Mary's feast in the Eucharist seemed to prevail. Already in the thirteenth century theological giants such as Albert the Great, Thomas Aquinas and Bonaventure championed the Assumption. During the sixteenth century the feast became the greatest of the Marian celebrations and one of the most prominent of the liturgical year.

The Defining of the Doctrine

Pius XII published the definition of the Assumption on the Feast of All Saints, 1950. He issued the statement in an Apostolic Constitution entitled *Munificentissimus Deus* (The Most Bountiful God).

The pressure for a definition had been mounting since 1849, even before the proclamation about the Immaculate Conception. Petitions for the dogma came from 113 cardinals, 2,505 bishops, 32,000 priests and male religious, 50,000 women religious and 8 million laypeople.

On May 1, 1946, the pope sent an encyclical letter (*Deiparae Virginis*) to the world's bishops. He asked them what they and their people thought about making the Assumption a dogma. Out of 1181 episcopal replies, 18 said it was not the right time for it and only 6 expressed doubt that it was part of revealed truth. The pope concluded that this was a vote of virtual unanimity, a positive expression of the ordinary teaching authority and a certain and firm proof that the Assumption was a revealed truth.

The text for the definition is both readable and inspiring. I would encourage you to get a copy for meditation, especially in preparing for the feast of the Assumption. The pope primarily uses arguments from the sermons of prominent Church fathers and theologians, the strong liturgical tradition, the popular devotion of the people especially in praying the fourth glorious mystery of the rosary.

Allow me to quote several of the citations the pope uses to support the doctrine:

> It was fitting that she who had kept her virginity intact in childbirth, should keep her own body free from all corruption even after death. It was fitting that she, who had carried the Creator as a child at her breast, should dwell in the divine tabernacles. It was fitting that the spouse whom the Father had taken to himself, should live in the divine mansions.
> —*Saint John Damascene,* On the Dormition

> You are she, who, as it is written, appears in beauty, and your virginal body is all holy, all chaste, entirely the dwelling place of God, so that it is henceforth completely exempt from dissolution into dust. Though still human, it is changed into the heavenly life of incorruptibility, truly living and glorious, undamaged and sharing in perfect life.
> —*Saint Germanus of Constantinople,* The Dormition

> Jesus did not wish to have the body of Mary corrupted after death, since it would have redounded to his own dishonor to have her virginal flesh, from which he had himself assumed flesh, reduced to dust.
> —*Saint Alphonsus Liguori,* The Glories of Mary

These are but three of a series of faith testimonies from earliest church history to modern times which Pius XII used to demonstrate the longstanding faith of the Church in the Assumption. Some of the persons quoted use what we would call the accommodated sense of Scripture, an approach less favored in our own times, but nonetheless compelling within the context.

For example, Saint Anthony of Padua explains the text, "Arise, O Lord into your resting place: you and the ark of your sanctification," by saying that just as Jesus has ascended into heaven, so Mary the Ark who bore him, "has risen up, since on this day the Virgin Mother has been taken up into her heavenly dwelling" (*Sermon on Assumption*).

Finally, the pope concludes his reflection with the words of the definition:

> By the authority of our Lord Jesus Christ, of the blessed
> Apostles Peter and Paul, and our own authority, we
> pronounce, declare and define it to be a divinely
> revealed dogma: that the Immaculate Mother of God,
> the ever Virgin Mary, having completed the course of
> her earthly life, was assumed into heavenly glory.

Ecumenical Difficulties

We have no problem with the Eastern Orthodox Church which believes in the Assumption and celebrates it liturgically. However that Church does not recognize the feast of the Immaculate Conception, because this doctrine was developed in the West as a result of the response to Pelagius and the meaning of original sin—an issue that has not preoccupied the East. At the same time the East does recognize Mary as sinless and All Holy.

On the other hand, the churches of the Reformation do have problems with the definitions of both Immaculate Conception and Assumption. Their objections are based mostly on the silence of Scripture about Mary's Assumption and a seeming lack of evidence of texts supporting the Immaculate Conception.

In the Anglican-Roman Catholic dialogue, some agreement was reached in a statement that said these two Marian dogmas are not just about Mary as an individual so much as a "sign" of salvation. Her entrance into heaven shows that humanity has already begun to share in the fruits of salvation won by her Son.

Jesuit Father Yarnold, a member of the dialogue listed seven points of agreement:

1. Mary's role is not to be so interpreted as to obscure the fact that Jesus Christ is the one mediator between God and man (See 1 Timothy 2:5).

2. Christian understanding of Mary is inseparably linked with the doctrines of Christ and the Church.

3. Mary, as Mother of God Incarnate, received a unique vocation.

4. God prepared her by his grace to be the Mother of the Savior, by whom she herself was redeemed.

5. She has already entered into the glory of heaven.

6. Both Churches honor Mary in the communion of saints and observe liturgical feasts in her honor.

7. Mary is a model of holiness, obedience and faith. She can therefore be regarded as a "prophetic figure of the Church."

—*Quoted by Christopher O'Donnell in his book,*
At Worship With Mary

Still there are many issues that divide Catholics from Anglicans, Methodists, Presbyterians and others. How can we reconcile the human mediation of Mary with the Lord Jesus as the one mediator? What is the nature of scriptural interpretation and how can it be used to support Marian doctrines? What is the meaning and role of the teaching authority of the Church? The dialogues with these various denominations consider these questions to be unresolved and in need of further discussion.

O'Donnell notes that one of the least developed areas of theology is the communion of saints. This is a communion of holy persons and holy gifts. In the Assumption Mary is fully united to her son in glory. She remains his mother. He remains her son. Their love has not vanished or diminished. It is now even more resplendent. Cardinal Suenens once said, "Jesus does not point out Mary and say, 'She used to be my mother.'" Mary is just as interested in our salvation as she was on earth. Catholics know and believe this. That is one reason why they say two billion Hail Marys every day. They expect Mary to help them and pray for them.

The Churches of the Reform could probe this doctrine more fruitfully than they have in the past. While they fret about Marian excess among some of the devout, they could direct their energies to the fact that they themselves pray for one another. If we can do it on earth, why not in heaven? There is no "wall of separation" between heaven and earth. We all freely seek the prayers of sinners on earth, for we are sinners all. Why not seek the intercession of the saints in heaven? Why not turn to the Queen of saints, God's own Mother?

Reflection

Archbishop Sheen made two unique applications of the doctrines of the Immaculate Conception and the Assumption to cultures of the age in which they were published. His insights continue to have relevance today.

The optimists announce inevitable progress. In the middle of the nineteenth century three thinkers established a modern agenda that excluded God:

✱ *People used Darwin's evolutionary theory to claim the origin of humans was in lower species. They went further and removed God as the origin of the human person.*

✳ *Marx developed an evolutionary theory of history in which there is inevitable progress and there will be more of it when there is less God or religion.*

✳ *John Stuart Mill envisioned the evolution of economics when we espouse a utilitarian view of freedom, the freedom to do what is useful, not what is right according to natural or divine law.*

These philosophies charmed so many because they were so optimistic and filled with promise.

Just when these three revolutionary views of humans, history and freedom captured the minds of millions, the Church proclaimed the Immaculate Conception. This doctrine says God is the origin of the human person. Humanity fell from grace and original holiness. History must be more than human progress without God: It is the setting for God's plan to save us in the Lord Jesus. Freedom divorced from saving grace can lead to sin, cruelty and anarchy.

While the culture talked about the soul in godless terms, the Church affirmed a doctrine of the soul that most aptly described the real condition of human nature. To an overly optimistic people the Church offered a realistic alternative. We are good but flawed; we may be lost but we can be redeemed. Our lives are, then, a history of lifelong moral and spiritual healing.

✳ *What do you do when faced with unfounded optimism? What are some examples of a foolish optimism you have known in your life?*

✳ *What spiritual resources do you bring to bear upon the challenges to your faith? How have you seen people misuse their freedom? How have you been able to help them?*

✳ *Why can it be legitimately said that the implications of the Immaculate Conception are realistic alternatives to a false sense of optimism and security?*

The right and wrong view of the body. In the middle of the twentieth century a French philosopher, Jean Paul Sartre, popularized existentialism—a pessimistic and despairing view of life. Two world wars, the Holocaust, the Bomb and the beginning of the Cold War seemed to justify his hopeless interpretation of human life.

His is a bleak world, with no God or future life. All we have between the present and our inevitable deaths is freedom, the act that tries to make some sense and meaning out of life. We have no one to help us. God may have made the world out of nothing; Sartre made nothing out of the world. Genesis taught we came from nothingness; Sartre taught we are going back to nothingness.

At the same time the followers of Freud were celebrating sexuality, not always in the way he may have intended. By the sixties the cult of the body and sex had taken hold of Western culture. The more that sex and the body were idolized the more there was a decline in marriage and family values.

Today we know the sad results all too well. There is widespread unease about what this means for our culture and its future. This is accompanied by the increase of drug use to deaden the unhappiness of the users. This development has caused a cultural pessimism that is the exact opposite of the unhindered optimism of the late nineteenth century.

The Church's definition of the Assumption in 1950 goes against the pessimism about life and the body which we have been experiencing in recent decades. The doctrine affirms the dignity of the body, a treasure so magnificent that it will reach even greater glory in heaven. We are not destined for "nothingness," but rather for the very fulfillment that every person longs for. Contrasted to contemporary pessimism, this doctrine is an optimistic, hope-filled act of confidence in the dignity of the body and its essential unity with the soul.

One of the unique contributions of Pope John Paul II to modern thinking is his theology of the body. He stresses its unity with the soul. We are more than a frail and tenuous union of soul and body; we are embodied souls. Deep within the body are the longings of the soul. Two elements are mysteriously united in one reality, the human person. His thinking extends and deepens our appreciation of the Assumption of Mary and our understanding of the future resurrection of our bodies. Seen this way, the Assumption of Mary is a canticle of praise for the fullness of the human person, an embodied soul.

* *Many have noted the increase of suicide among our young people. In your experience what would you say are the reasons for this? What accounts for the unfounded pessimism among many in contemporary society?*

* *Who are some outstanding people in modern life that give the world a sense of hope? Why have they succeeded? Who are people you know that have discovered the grounds for hope in their lives? What is their secret?*

* *Why is the mystery of the Assumption relevant to our quest for hope in a troubled world? Why is it important to see ourselves as embodied souls rather than a loose connection of body and soul?*

Prayer

All powerful and ever-living God,
you raised the sinless Virgin Mary,
mother of your Son,
body and soul to the glory of heaven.
May we see heaven as our final goal
and come to share her glory. Amen.
—*Prayer for Feast of Assumption*

Filippo Lippi (and workshop)
THE NATIVITY (detail depicting the Madonna)
1470
Museo Civico, Prato, Italy

CHAPTER EIGHT

❀

Christ's Disciple

*T*he Blessed Virgin does not disillusion

any of the profound expectations

of the men and women of our time

but offers them the perfect model

of the disciple of the Lord.

—*Marialis Cultus*

Look at the Star—Call on Mary

And the virgin's name was Mary.

We will dwell a while on this name which is, rightly interpreted, "Star of the Sea," and is therefore admirably appropriate to the Virgin Mother.... She is...that glorious star which arose from Jacob, and which casts its radiance over the whole world....

O you who find yourself tossed about by the storms of life, turn not your eyes from the brightness of this Star, if you would not be overwhelmed by its boisterous waves. If the winds of temptations rise, if you fall among the rocks of tribulations, look up at the Star, call on Mary. If anger, covetousness, or other passions beat on the vessel of your soul, look up at Mary. If you begin to sink in the gulf of melancholy and despair, think on Mary. In dangers, in distress, in perplexities, think on Mary, call on Mary.

Let her not depart from your lips, let her not depart from your heart, and, that you may win the suffrage of her prayers, never depart from the example of her life.

Following her, you will never go astray; when you implore her aid, you will never yield to despair; thinking on her, you will not err; under her patronage you will never wander; beneath her protection you will not fear; she being your guide, you will not weary; if she be your propitious Star, you will arrive safely in port, and experience for yourself the truth of the words, "And the virgin's name was Mary."

...Let us, then, gaze in silent contemplation on that which words are powerless to explain.

—*Saint Bernard*, Homily on the Annunciation

I have always found these exuberant words of Saint Bernard to be the language of love. He was Mary's medieval troubadour, singing her praises. His homily still leaps up off the page, filled with his contagious affection for her. But, while Bernard makes Mary a Star, he never forgets that Jesus is the Sun. The only reason Bernard gives Mary so much attention is that she draws us to the Lord

Jesus, our destiny and Savior.

He is our King; Mary is our petitioner on our behalf. Since we so often walk in the night of distress, anxiety, insecurity and fear, we have a Star named Mary, who will guide us to the Sun, Jesus, our final port in the storms of life.

Bernard's homily is part of a series of talks he gave in Advent. They are called the *Missus Est* sermons and several portions of them appear in the *Liturgy of the Hours*. They are meditations on the mystery of the Incarnation.

While his words are weighted with sound doctrine, they are songs of love more than academic talk. Bernard was a man fully unashamed to speak from his heart about Our Lady who was obviously so important to him. He was more than an orator using techniques to dazzle his listeners. In fact Bernard surpasses that kind of speaking. He doesn't want to mesmerize us. He intends to open up our hearts and let our love flow as abundantly as his own.

He commands our affections, wakes them up and throws them outward. Just read his sermons on how to love God and you will experience what I mean. And when he talks about Mary, we cannot be indifferent to her. He provides the intimacy we need to open ourselves to her so she can help us to love her Son.

When I was a student at Lumen Vitae in Brussels, Belgium, in 1962 to 1963, I often heard people use the expression, "Oh, that's so medieval." They used this term to disparage whatever was being said or done as out-of-date or irrelevant to the modern world.

I resisted this reference to the Middle Ages mainly because I was—and am—a great admirer of the faith and fruits of medieval life. I love their Gothic cathedrals, their tapestries and illuminated Bibles. I like the stories they told and the colorful lives of their saints, such as Catherine of Siena and Joan of Arc. I remain humbled and impressed with the genius of their thinkers like Aquinas and spiritual writers like Bonaventure and Bernard.

Of course, I knew as well as anyone the dark side of

medieval life, its violence, its passions, its injustices, its cruelties in the Crusades and the treatment of heretics. But then, who is without sin? It seemed to me that using history against itself is unwise and not as rewarding as looking into our past and seeing what treasures have survived to benefit our contemporary world.

I remember my discomfort with the dismissive comment about medievalism because I believed it was unfair and short-sighted. I recall it here because it was in the Middle Ages that Mary came into her own in the awareness of the universal Church. The Church Fathers of the fourth century had initiated the theology of Mary. It took the Middle Ages to explore her role in liturgy and devotion for the benefit of our faith in Christ.

The medieval Mary was a royal person, a queen who reigned in heavenly glory and earthly majesty. Today, our Church has discovered a different, down-to-earth aspect of Mary, the human disciple of Jesus. Here we have an angle to contemplate all the images of Mary that make up her complex and attractive presence for us.

How Is Mary a Disciple?

For centuries Mary has served the Church as a model of holiness. Each age finds in her a new way to follow Christ. Changing times bring new perceptions. In our culture, for example, the role of women has evolved. In the Christian family today we recognize that women share equally with men in the management of the household.

Today many women have occupations outside the home. Women have entered political life, run for office and attained the highest levels of public government. Women are highly visible in the professions as lawyers, writers, doctors, researchers, scientists, journalists, editors and psychologists. In the business world, women manage businesses and chair boards and advise people on their investments.

How can Mary be a model for these women? How can

a woman who lived in the narrow horizons of a tiny home in an obscure village two thousand years ago be relevant to the modern woman—or the modern man for that matter? These are questions that need honest attention and prayerful reflection. Answers will not come easily nor quickly, but there are some principles which can shed light on the solutions.

The first is that we are not expected to imitate Mary in terms of her social and cultural context. We are not asked to live like first-century people who never took a plane, used a computer or shopped at a mall. That would be anachronistic. It would be playacting to try to physically reproduce Nazareth and its social customs in our lives today. That is what theme villages, such as Williamsburg, Virginia, do. But they are museums, not living realities.

Mary fully and responsibly accepted the will of God in a town with narrow, winding and dusty streets. We must do it on highways, high-speed trains, elevators, office towers and suburbs or city neighborhoods. Mary heard the Word of God and kept it in a small mud-brick house with no labor-saving devices. We must obey God's Word in apartments, townhouses, tenements and high-rises equipped with modern conveniences to ease our way.

Mary was the first and most perfect of Christ's disciples because the driving force of her life was love and service. She managed with a simple wardrobe when compared to moderns whose closets are overstocked with fashions. Nonetheless we, too, can have souls motivated by love and service just like her. We are not called upon to replicate a culture. We are challenged to reproduce discipleship.

The second principle is to separate culture-bound popular images of Mary that have appeared in writings and customs about her from the authentic biblical and doctrinal truths about her. Just as we are not expected to replace Main Street, U.S.A., with Main Street, Nazareth, so no one should demand that popular helps to Marian devotion tied to another set of customs be our way of doing it.

Our devotion to Mary must be based on Scripture and

authentic doctrinal development. I hope I have shown you in the previous chapters how slowly and conscientiously doctrinal teachings about Mary have been drawn from the biblical data. Just read again the struggle over Mary as Theotokos. Succeeding generations have indeed created a host of images and customs to accompany doctrinal development.

Our ancestors in the faith have contemplated Mary as virgin, mother, wife, the ideal woman and an outstanding example of how to live the gospel. The outward expressions of these ways of looking at Mary are often tied to a given culture, but may not be suitable for a new generation. There should be continuity in the essentials, but not necessarily in temporary expressions.

The third guiding principle is to express scriptural and doctrinal truths about Mary in our own culture. We need the guidance of the Holy Spirit to help us validly integrate our faith with the contemporary scene. How can Mary mirror the expectations of men and women of our day?

Those of us with important decisions to make can be inspired by Mary's courage when she is called upon to make the most important decision anyone ever faced. The decision to accept the Incarnation was greater than any other choice made by any man or woman in history; its consequence affected the whole world for all of history. Mary chose the virginity that prepared her for the conception and birth of Jesus. She did not reject the values of marriage. But she did make a courageous decision to consecrate herself entirely to the love of God. Great choices require profound courage. It's the courage Mary witnesses. The result is an undivided heart, a total love for God. Choice and decision-making are popular terms in our culture.

It is true that certain forms of Christian art and writing have tended to portray Mary as a timid and submissive woman. Yet in her Magnificat she joyfully noted that God will rescue the humble and oppressed and remove the powerful from their "thrones." Mary was a woman who stood with the poor and oppressed because she was one of them, a woman who fled a murderous politician and went with her husband and child into exile. She knew poverty and suffering and stood proudly and bravely at the cross when virtually all of Jesus' closest friends ran away. This is no timid and fearful woman.

Even when the apostles had gained some renewed nerve and confidence after Easter, they still needed Mary in the upper room as they awaited the mystery of Pentecost. Mary does not appear there as a shy recluse, modestly sitting at the margin of the community. She is firmly in the middle of the community, holding them together until they could be molded into a courageous spiritual force by the power of the Holy Spirit.

Mary responds very well to the expectations and hopes of modern men and women. She shows us how to be true disciples of the Lord Jesus. She walks with us and before us as we fulfill our calling to create a just and peaceful world, but also as we pilgrimage to our final community in heaven. She is the disciple that calls us to bring justice to the oppressed and love to each individual that is in need. She is the disciple who loved Jesus with all her heart and can teach us to do the same. We need always to be reminded that we have the gift of Mary to help us glorify God and be committed to lives which are in total conformity to God's will.

A fourth guiding principle is to follow the example of Mary as a model of the Church at worship. Pope Paul VI dwelt on this topic in his *Marialis Cultus* (On Devotion to the Blessed Virgin Mary). Discipleship includes worship and the attitudes which accompany it. Mary embodies the spiritual attitudes which we need when celebrating the divine mysteries. The Church calls us to be like her in seeking intimacy with Christ through whom we worship the Father.

The attentive woman. Mary was the attentive woman who received God's Word with faith. She conceived Christ in faith before she conceived him in the flesh. In the second chapter of this book, we considered Mary's pilgrimage of faith, the various ways in which her attentiveness to God's address increased her faith. At liturgy we are expected to come with the same kind of faithful attentiveness, especially in the liturgy of the Word whereby God speaks to us and calls us to open our hearts to the sacrament.

The woman of prayer. Mary is a witness of prayer. In three wonderful scriptural scenes, Mary exemplifies powerful moments of prayer. In front of Elizabeth she sings the Magnificat, a hymn of praise for the Incarnation. By mingling Old Testament texts and her own sentiments, Mary recaptures the history of salvation and provides the Church with a canticle that is sung every evening in the universal Church. The second scene is Cana where Mary intercedes with Jesus to begin his saving ministry.

In the third scene at Pentecost, she prays with the infant Church for the coming of the Spirit. Since the Assumption Mary continues to pray for each of us. Our ability to participate actively in the liturgy is closely connected to our capacity for prayer, which needs to be nourished each day. We cannot expect to arrive at liturgy and begin praying if we have not acquired the habit and attitude of prayer on a daily basis. Otherwise our presence at liturgy will be mostly mechanical.

The woman who presents offerings. Mary is the Woman of the Offerings. From the moment the Incarnate Word existed in this world, the Son of God was offering himself to the Father to save us from sin and give us divine life. When Mary brings her child to the temple for the Presentation of the Lord, she was continuing his own offering. It is in the sacrificial offering of the Son to the Father that our redemption is accomplished. Every Eucharist is a sacramental reliving of this divine offering.

Scripture makes clear that this offering would include Christ's death on the Cross. Even at the Presentation, Simeon's words about Jesus being the source of the rise and fall of many, and of a sword that would pierce the soul of Mary, prophetically refer to the Cross. Guided by the Spirit, this has been the Church's intuition of the meaning of the encounter with Simeon. At Calvary Mary united herself with a mother's heart to Christ's sacrifice. She offered him to the Father. And she offered herself in union with him.

The offering of which we speak is often called sacrificial love. In Christ, this became a redemptive act. We are called to acquire this attitude both of offering the great gift of Jesus to the Father—and of offering ourselves in union with him. Of course we need to practice sacrificial love in our daily lives to obtain the inner attitude that enables us to enter into the mystery of the liturgy more deeply. This demands firm faith and fiery love from us.

Now we have seen four principles that can guide us to be disciples like Mary:

1. Imitate Mary in her interior attitudes, not her social and cultural context.

2. Base our devotion to Mary on Scripture and authentic doctrinal development.

3. Discover ways to express scriptural and doctrinal truths about Mary in our contemporary world.

4. Study the role of Mary as a model of the Church at worship. Here we see her as the woman of attentive faith, the woman of prayer, and the woman of sacrificial offerings. How we apply these principles will depend on our own personalities and circumstances.

The Marian Teaching of Vatican II

During the preparation for Vatican II there was pressure to create a major document about the Virgin Mary. The Fathers settled for a chapter about Mary within the document on the Church (*Lumen Gentium*). I think this is a good place to offer you a summary of its teachings because they form the foundation for understanding Mary's discipleship.

The Council Fathers synthesized the doctrines about Mary within the mystery of Christ and the Church. This method followed the approach of the early Church Fathers who preferred the model of the history of salvation as the way to organize the teachings. They made clear that Mary is not a marginal figure in faith and theology. By her intimate participation in the history of salvation, Mary "in a certain way unites and mirrors within herself the central truths of faith" (*Church*).

The other organizing theme for presenting Mary was her relationship to the Trinity. Through Jesus, Mary has a special relationship to God the Father. Saint Paul informed the Galatians that God sent his Son, born of a woman, in the fullness of time (cf. Galatians 4:4-5). Mary became the handmaid of the Lord by opening her heart and body to God's Word, and thereby gave life to the world. By grace she became the Mother of God. Because of her unique mission, God the Father preserved her from original sin. The Father willed that "the consent of the predestined mother should precede the incarnation" ("The Church").

The Council proceeded to draw five ways in which Mary is related to Christ.

1. *Mary is the greatest outcome of redemption.* Of all the people saved by Christ, Mary is the most outstanding. She is saved in a sublime manner by the merits of her Son. The Fathers, the liturgy and the Magisterium have called Mary, in the order of grace, "the daughter of her Son" (Council of Toledo).

2. *Mary is the Mother of God.* Having said her yes to the angel, by the power of the Holy Spirit she conceived and gave birth to the Son of God. She remained a virgin and there was no intervention of any man. She fed him, took care of him and educated him (cf. "The Church").

3. *Mary is the faithful servant.* Impeded by no sin, she gave herself with all her heart to God's saving will. She devoted herself completely to the work of her Son, serving the task of redemption by God's grace (cf. "The Church").

4. *Mary is the cooperator with the Redeemer.* "The Fathers see Mary as not merely passively engaged by God, but as freely cooperating in the work of man's salvation through faith and obedience" ("The Church").

I should add here that there have been numerous petitions to the Vatican to define Mary as co-redemptrix as part of the Millennium Jubilee in the year 2000. The Holy See has replied by saying that viewing Mary as cooperator with the Redeemer seems to be the preferred approach.

It was noted that this is how Pope John Paul II, citing the Council, has chosen to speak of Mary in this regard. "In an utterly singular way, she cooperated by her obedience, faith, hope and burning charity in the Savior's work of restoring supernatural life to souls" ("The Church").

5. *Mary is the disciple.* When Jesus praised those who hear the Word of God and keep it, for they are his mother, brother and sister (Mark 3:35), he would apply that commendation primarily to his mother ("The Church").

Mary's connection with the Holy Spirit comes through Christ and rounds out her relationship with the Trinity. If anyone has ever been more effectively a Temple of the Spirit it was certainly Mary. She has often been pictured as the Ark of the Covenant. That Ark was the sacred icon of Israel upon which was often seen the shining cloud called the "glory" (*shekinah* and *kabod* in Hebrew). This was the way in which God made himself visible and experienced by the people. The Ark bore the divine presence. Golden angels, mounted on the Ark, were sculptured kneeling with heads bowed in adoration of the divine glory.

Luke's Gospel says that the Spirit would conceive the child in the womb of Mary by overshadowing her like a cloud—similar to the cloud-glory that dwelt upon the Ark. At the Visitation, the Spirit worked through Mary to impart the gifts of the Savior to the child in Elizabeth's womb. In the days before Pentecost Mary joined the disciples in "prayerfully imploring the gift of the Spirit, who had already overshadowed her in the Annunciation" ("The Church").

The Council Fathers proceeded to outline Mary's relation to the Church. We will consider their teachings on this doctrine in our final chapter on Mary as Mother of the Church.

Reflection

I have outlined the principles which guide us in forming points of contact with Mary within the scope of our own culture. Now I suggest three ways in which we can practice discipleship of Christ with Mary as our guide: Purity of Heart, Obedience of Faith and Simplicity of Life.

Purity of heart. The Fathers of the fourth century and the saints of the medieval period found inspiration in Mary's physical virginity and bodily chastity. In our days when prime-time TV, summer movies and pop music generate images of sexual promiscuity, it would seem that Mary's physical purity would be our best response to this devaluing of the human body. I believe this can be a productive opening to countering the collapse of sexual morality.

I also think that a singular motivation can be sought by getting in touch with Mary's purity of heart which excluded all sin and involved a total dedication to God. Mary is the supreme example of the undivided heart. Her purity of heart caused her not only to avoid sexual sin, but any kind of sin. She is a sinless woman. Her moral horizon excluded all possibilities of alienation from God. She made a fundamental option for God and lived it concretely in each act of her life. She lived morally what she believed in her heart.

Her purity of heart was more than a mere avoidance of sin, it was also a serene cultivation of the virtues. Her heart was like a garden where the sins were never allowed to grow and in which the flowers and trees of virtue were carefully tended. Her inner drive to God was far more an attraction to those strengths and powers that would ennoble her embodied soul than preoccupation with sin. In our language, she understood that her psychic energies were best spent on faith, hope and love along with the human virtues.

I believe that we should be as impassioned as she was to avoid every sin, not just those of impurity. I also think that we would be wise to put our energies into a joyful practice of all the virtues, a positive vision of these powers that project us into the heart of God. I know that then we would abandon a moral minimalism that confines us to battling some passions while forgetting the whole range of our weaknesses. We would also experience ourselves as growing with inner powers that drive us to God and away from that which diminishes us.

Now Mary did this with full awareness that grace was the secret of her purity of heart. The Spirit was accomplishing this marvel in her because of her cooperation. We should realize that our own future is a matter of grace. We need to become aware that the Spirit wants to transform us with our wide-awake cooperation. We have the call to become saints who are sinners making progress. The purity of heart that will make us delightful disciples is the victory of grace.

* *What is your own vision of purity of heart? Why do you think it is important? How does it compare to our culture's loss of a moral compass?*

* *While Mary's perpetual virginity and bodily purity are enduring sources of inspiration for us today, why is her*

purity of heart a singularly useful model of discipleship for contemporary people?

✳ *It has been said that the right attitude is the best preparation for the right aptitude. How would you apply this idea to the role of purity of heart in your life?*

Obedience of faith. A second way that Mary models discipleship is her obedience of faith. It's not easy to sell obedience to the modern sensibility. It has overtones of an undesirable passivity and submissiveness where we leave our brains at the door. It seems to justify arbitrary use of authority or mindlessly "doing one's duty." It appears to expect conformity without any questions. It treats questioning itself as a form of disloyalty. If we proceed to connect obedience with faith it seems as though we are putting a divine stamp of approval on acts that are not fully human.

Some of these views of obedience survive from a time when some authority figures probably had too much authority and, being sinful, misused their role. Whatever the reasons, I think we need to disentangle false forms of obedience from the true ones. Obedience involves two acts— listening and doing. The short-sighted practice of obedience stresses the doing and minimizes the listening. Real obedience includes intelligence and responsible freedom.

I have frequently called your attention to Mary as a listener to the Word. Mary heard the Word attentively, prayerfully and deeply. Hers was more than a quick, superficial "Yes, sir" to the surface of what she heard. She listened with her heart more than with her ears. The brevity of the Annunciation scene should not deceive us. Even there she slowed down the interaction between herself and the angel.

She drew the message into her heart and looked at it with her whole self. She really listened to the Word with all the attentiveness of her contemplative being. For her, God was more than a commander barking orders. God was a lover asking for a response of love. Her faith revealed this to her and alerted her to the seriousness and joyfulness of what she was invited to do.

This is the obedience that suits our times quite well. It's as modern as any genuinely enlightened attitude. Our obedience is not meant to be a rush to behavior. It is first of all an exercise in contemplative listening. It means a gathering of our inner selves to really hear what God is asking of us. Our faith makes possible this dialogue with God. Our membership in the community of the Church assures us that we will hear with an ecclesial heart. Faith is not lone-wolf behavior. This is a kind of hearing that slows down the pace of life so that authentic listening can happen. When we have become accustomed to this approach then the obedience of faith can be a fulfilling form of discipleship.

✻ *What has been your experience of obedience? How has your view of obedience developed as you matured into adulthood? What would you consider to be inadequate ways of obeying?*

✻ *How does modern individualism color people's concept of obedience? In your "obedience of faith," how much is hearing God's Word and how much is quick conformity or nonconformity in action?*

✻ *How could you "slow down" the listening and doing steps in the obedience of faith? Why should you do so? How could Mary's witness help you?*

Simplicity of life. The complexity of modern life is here to stay. Nostalgia for the simplicity of a pre-technological culture is unrealistic. But we can still simplify our lives within the new context. How this will be accomplished depends on the situation of each person and family. Mary lived a simple life in a world where simplicity was easier if we just think of the relative sameness of a quiet village in biblical times.

Nevertheless, she had some extraordinary complexities

to deal with in that social tranquility. Rebellious currents against Roman oppression created an edge in social awareness. Her own situation was unique. She was a virgin in a marital household. She had conceived a son in a miraculous manner. While we have no scriptural evidence, nor need we be overimaginative regarding the thoughts of the families of Joseph and Mary, we can at least say that Mary faced one of the most complex situations a young woman could have.

Matters grew more complicated when suddenly, at the age of thirty, Jesus embarked on an extraordinary public life filled with controversy, celebrity and mixed reviews of adulation and rejection. The danger of his truth drew the attention of the highest religious and political authorities in the land. The family and neighbors seemed perplexed and upset by him.

Mary needed to maintain a simplicity of vision in the midst of a mounting set of conflicting events. After thirty years of contemplating the mystery of her son in the dreamlike sameness of a biblical town, she watched him be swept up in historic events that possessed the ebb and flow of an ocean full of conflict, full of pain. At some level, with a mother's intuition, she may have known it would turn out this way. That strange prophecy of Simeon may well have lingered in her memory, alternately suppressed and yet admitted.

Her habit of simplicity needed to be exercised more aggressively as Jesus moved inexorably to the final and fatal encounter with those who would plan his death. No matter how bewildering it all became, Mary could never allow circumstances to cause her to swerve from her simple vision of the will of God for her son—and for herself as well. Simplicity of life had its counterpart of simplicity of insight in the deepest wells of her heart. Whether alone in her home or surrounded by a few friends at the cross, Mary carried the virtue of simplicity which laid aside all contingent factors and concentrated on the one thing necessary— the will of God and the world's salvation.

For us, simplicity of life includes a modest life-style, but more importantly, it means keeping a clear idea of what our lives are all about, who we are, where we came from and where we are going. It is essentially tied to our understanding of what God's will is for us and the determination, with God's grace, to remain faithful to it.

✳ *What would you need to do to live a more simple life-style? Why would you want to do it? Who are people you admire who have achieved this goal?*

✳ *At the level of simplicity, what do you find most appealing in the witness of Mary? Why is it important for discipleship?*

✳ *What could prompt you to sit back and acquire simplicity in both your outer and inner life? When have you known the pleasures of simplicity?*

Prayer

Lord our God,
through the Blessed Virgin Mary
you have shown us the example of a disciple,
who is faithful to the words of life;
open our hearts to receive your saving word,
so that by the power of the Holy Spirit
it may speak to us in our daily lives
and bring forth a rich harvest of holiness. Amen.
—*From the Mass of Mary, Disciple of the Lord*

Salvador Dali
THE MADONNA OF PORT LLIGAT (First Version)
1949
Patrick and Beatrice Haggerty Museum of Art
Marquette University, Milwaukee, Wisconsin
Gift of Mr. and Mrs. Ira Haupt, 59.9

CHAPTER NINE

❀

Mary of the Appearances

"What do you want of me?" asked Lucia.

"I am the Lady of the Rosary.

Let them say the rosary every day."

—*Final Appearance at Fatima*

"Papa, papa! The Madonna is weeping!"

> I began the Mass about 8:15 in the morning. The statue
> was in a sort of basket. It began to weep as we were
> saying the *Salve Regina*. My sister was braver than I
> was; she touched the statue, and some blood came off
> on her finger. I did not have the courage to do that. But
> I saw the tear drop very slowly, ending at the foot of the
> statue.
> —*Girolamo Grillo, Bishop of Civitavecchia*

On February 2, 1995, six-year-old Jessica Gregori was play-
ing in the backyard of her home in Civitavecchia, a seaside
town fifty miles north of Rome. Her father, Fabio, had built
a small shrine to house a statue of Mary which the local
pastor brought to him from Medjugorje. It was a gift meant
to celebrate Fabio's conversion back to Catholicism after his
years as a Jehovah's Witness.

The sixteen-inch statue was similar to hundreds of
other images of Mary. But on that extraordinary afternoon,
the playful Jessica shouted, "Papa, papa! The Madonna is
weeping!" Jessica's parents rushed out to the yard. They,
too, saw the tears of blood coming from the eyes of the
statue.

The news spread quickly, bringing the neighbors and
curiosity seekers to see the statue. Police were needed to
control the crowd. It was too much for Fabio Gregori and
his family. He packaged the little statue and took it to
Bishop Girolamo Grillo. It seemed to be the most practical
thing to do.

Bishop Grillo reluctantly accepted the statue. He had
heard about it and had expressed disbelief. His diocese had
been filled with talk about miraculous happenings and
even the practice of Satanism. He was known as a thoughtful bishop, inclined to be wary of spectacular religious phenomena.

But one month later, while celebrating Mass for his sister, his nephew and two nuns, he saw the statue weep tears

of blood. They all saw it. The bishop could no longer be a disinterested prelate; he was an involved witness.

Other than to inform the Vatican, he resolved to keep quiet about the experience. Generally he did so, but on April 5, 1995, he admitted on a television interview that he had seen the statue weep. Millions heard his story. The bishop convened an inter-disciplinary commission of scientists and theologians to investigate the statue. It concluded that no tricks were used, that the blood was genuine and that there was no rational explanation for it.

The bishop then installed the statue behind bullet-proof glass in a parish church for public viewing. Thousands have flocked to see it. It has been reported that a number of healings and conversions have occurred. Bishop Grillo now awaits a judgment from the Vatican and the outcome of an investigation of over fifty claimed healings.

If this is an authentic divine intervention and a true manifestation of Mary, its purpose will be to strengthen the faith of believers and spread the faith to others. The event should call people to a deeper prayer life, a noticeable moral conversion and active participation in the sacraments, especially the Eucharist. It should nourish faith in the Holy Trinity, Christ and the Eucharist and God's plan for our salvation from sin and the gift of divine life.

In the approved appearances of Mary, such as at Lourdes and Fatima, our Blessed Mother invites us to a renewed faith in the Gospels and the authentic teachings of the Church. She asks us to hear the Word of God attentively and witness it in our lives. She urges us to be prayerful people.

The focus in her life was on doing the Father's will, giving Christ to the world, praying under the guidance of the Spirit and living in the heart of the Church. She does nothing differently in her genuine appearances. Mary just asks us to do what she did.

This is the framework for pondering the numerous new alleged appearances of Mary in recent times. We are all aware of accepted visions of Mary at Lourdes, Fatima and

La Sallette. Now we should look at more recent claims. I will cite three of them here and then present some guidelines which the Church uses to determine whether or not such appearances are real.

Ray Doiron's Witness

In January 1993, a retired bread-delivery man, Ray Doiron, was preparing for sleep. A beautiful woman appeared to him at his home in Renault, Illinois. Dressed in white, she told him, "I come to you as a loving mother." The humble man wondered why. "I picked you because you are the least apt instrument. Therefore, people will know that this is not your word." She asked Ray to urge people to pray for peace, reject evil and welcome God.

Ray was a regular visitor to Our Lady of the Snows shrine in Belleville for twenty years. After his first vision at home, he began to have the visions at the shrine. People heard of this and now pack the amphitheater to pray with him. Father William Clark, director of the shrine says, "I can't claim what he does or doesn't see. I'll tell you what I see. I see six thousand people coming to pray, which is a very good thing."

Medjugorje

In 1981, six young peasants reported a visit from the Virgin in Medjugorje, Yugoslavia. The visionaries say Mary has been delivering messages there almost every day since then. Over eleven million pilgrims have visited the site. Hundreds of people have claimed physical healings and countless others speak of spiritual and moral conversions. None of the miraculous cures have been verified by the exacting standards used at Lourdes.

The local bishop, Pavao Zanic, has not given official approval. He has claimed, "The Madonna has never said anything at Medjugorje." The Vatican has initiated its own investigation of the matter. Father Castellano Cervera, an expert in Marian studies and a consultant to the Vatican, judges the millions of pilgrims to be seekers, not just lookers. "It seems clear to me that one can go to Medjugorje, just as one goes to any sanctuary, to deepen one's Christian life." As of this writing, no formal judgment has been made by the Church as to the authenticity of the Marian appearances at Medjugorje.

Lubbock Appearances—A Case Study

In 1988, three parishioners of Saint John Neumann parish in Lubbock, Texas, said they were receiving messages from Mary during their daily recitation of the rosary at the church. On August 15, the Feast of the Assumption, twelve thousand people came to the parish for Mass. The visionaries claimed Mary appeared to them along with Christ in the midst of celestial phenomena during the Eucharist. Some people testified they saw the sun spinning and pulsating, rosaries changing color, healings and Polaroid pictures of the gates of heaven in the sky.

Bishop Michael Sheehan convened a committee to investigate the matter. Father Frederick Jelly, O.P., chaired the committee and presented the final report. He noted many positive aspects of the experience but said he and his committee failed to find anything miraculous.

They studied the Rosary Messages (as they were called) received by the two women and one man during the recitation of the rosary at the church. These messages were generally within the boundary of sound Catholic teaching. Some of the messages presented an angry God speaking in such strident language that the committee questioned their claim to divine origin. The committee concluded that these messages did not come from a miraculous source, but were rather inner thoughts prompted by the recipients' spiritual reading, sermons they heard, or the result of their meditations and contemplative prayer.

Their messages appear to be coming out of a normal prayer life and have touched the lives of many. There were many notable spiritual conversions in terms of the number of confessions heard, the return of significant numbers of people to the Church and important reconciliations within families. The committee was moved by the deep devotion to Mary which is in evidence at the parish.

Bishop Sheehan posed three questions to the committee. Here are the questions and the replies of the committee.

1. *Are there miracles or not?*
   a. The messages are not miraculous in the strict sense of deriving from sources beyond natural explanation. But they were channels of grace in the sense there were clear pastoral results in confessions, spiritual healings and renewal.
   b. Concerning the reported phenomena on August 15 (sun spinning and pulsating and moon changing colors, healings and the reports of many who said they could look at the sun without eye damage), beyond the some-250 written testimonies received, we were not equipped to submit these phenomena or their aftereffects to rigid scientific analysis...The limited phenomena we have been able to examine with sufficient analysis admit of natural explanations. Many other phenomena were submitted, and we had neither the time nor the resources to investigate them fully.

2. *Should the rosary messages be promoted?*

If the "rosary messages" are conveyed as the pious meditations of good people and not private revelations miraculously produced, the content of Mary Constancio's and Mike Slate's messages may be shared with others.

3. *What is prudent for the parish to do in the future regarding the devotions?*
   a. The rosary devotions should be allowed to continue.
   b. Any rosary messages that might be received in the future should be submitted for the bishop's approval be-

fore being published.

c. A bishop's committee should be set up as advisory to the pastor of St. John Neumann Parish relative to these matters.

d. The subsequent pastoring of this whole affair is of concern to us, and so people must be particularly warned against the harmful effects of sun gazing (Three people suffered eye damage) as well as an otherworldly spirit that leads people to abandon their sources of economic support (cf. 2 Thessalonians 3:6-12).

e. In pastoring the application of the messages, care should be taken that the piety engendered not be individualistic (e.g., bringing flowers to Mary) but lead to the creation of real community and social concerns.

—Cf. *Statement on "Rosary Messages" in Lubbock,* Origins

I think you can agree that this committee showed great sympathy to all people concerned in this event. They helped people to see that God's grace normally works through the ordinary events of life. They drew the participants to reflect on the regular sources of spirituality— Church teaching, the celebration of the liturgy, community formation, prayer, meditation and social concern. They cautioned them against damaging their eyes by sun-gazing or imprudently giving up their jobs and property because they thought the end of the world was about to occur. They encouraged the continuance of the recitation of the rosary along with an advisory board to supervise any future, apparent revelations.

Norms for Evaluating Apparitions

In the eighteenth century the Church adopted a guideline by Prospero Lambertini (the future Pope Benedict XIV) about private revelations that has proved useful and prudent.

> It is necessary to know that the approbation given by
> the Church to a private revelation is nothing other than
> a permission accorded, after attentive examination, to
> communicate this revelation for the instruction and
> good of the faithful. To such revelations, even those
> approved by the Church, one must not accord the
> assent of Catholic faith. It is necessary only, according to
> the law of prudence, to give to them the assent of
> human belief to the degree that such revelations appear
> probably and piously credible.
> —*Catherine O'Dell*, Those Who Saw Her

Regarding approved apparitions, Lambertini advised that believers could refuse to believe in apparitions, "provided this is done with suitable modesty, for good reasons and without contempt." In other words Catholics should remember that apostolic tradition, sacred Scripture and the teachings of the Magisterium provide us with the essential message of salvation. These teachings call for the assent of religious faith. Private revelations are useful when they help strengthen that faith. But private revelations themselves only require "human faith," that is, reason. If our reason asks us not to accept them, we should do so "with suitable modesty and without contempt." (See also the *Catechism of the Catholic Church*, 67, about private revelation.)

Having said this, we need to see how the Church discerns whether or not a true vision of Christ, Mary, a saint or an angel has occurred. What is a bishop to do when confronted with such an event in his diocese? What norms guide him? In our case study we saw the answers to Bishop Sheehan's questions. What were the principles used by the committee to help them arrive at their conclusions? There are positive and negative signs. Taken together they form a set of norms for discerning how authentic a given vision is.

When a Catholic claims to have a vision, this news should be brought to the attention of the bishop. Once it seems clear that there is a strong probability of an apparition, it is the bishop's responsibility to initiate a process for determining the truth of the experience. He should expect that his investigating team will interview the visionary and possible eyewitnesses. They should visit the place of the alleged visions. They should interview all persons who could provide the needed information so that actual facts can be established. Their probe may by guided by the following signs.

Positive Signs

∗ *What are the personal qualities of the person claiming to have the apparition? Is the person mentally stable, honest, sincere and morally upright? Does the person have an attitude of obedience to Church authority? Would the person be willing to return to the normal practice of the faith and Christian life? The persons involved should be psychologically balanced, honest, respectful to Church authority and living a good moral life.*

∗ *What is the nature of the content of the message received in the private revelation? Is it theologically and morally true and free from error? No doctrinal errors may be attributed to God, Mary or a saint.*

∗ *What are the results of the apparition? Are they positive? The apparition should result in sound devotion and spiritual fruits such as prayer, real religious and moral conversions and the witness of love, mercy and justice.*

Negative Signs

∗ *Is there real ground for doubt about the occurrence? Are there natural reasons for the event that exclude the need to attribute the occasion to supernatural causes?*

∗ *Does the message of the visionary contain doctrinal error attributed to God, Mary or a saint? Is the visionary attaching some personal agenda to the message that could not be attributed to a divine source?*

* *Is the visionary making money on the event? Authentic seers refuse any kind of financial advantage. Bernadette resolutely refused all gifts and monies that people tried to impose on her.*

* *Has the visionary and followers engaged in any kind of immoral act at the time or on the occasion of the alleged apparition?*

* *Is the visionary delusional or psychopathic? There should be no psychopathic tendency in the person which might enter into the alleged miraculous event and no psychosis or collective hysteria of some type.*

These signs are not exhaustive. They must be applied cumulatively to the event. They should converge in the process of discerning the miraculous character of the apparition. It is not easy to apply these norms to what is usually a complex matter. Determining the real facts to arrive at a prudent judgment is a difficult task. If you would like to read further about these norms, please consult: "Discerning the Miraculous: Norms for Judging Apparitions and Private Revelations," by Father Frederick M. Jelly, O.P., *Marian Studies*, Volume XLIV, 1993, Marian Library, Dayton, Ohio.

I hope you don't think I am trying to make you suspicious of visions and appearances of Mary in the sense that I am implying such events no longer occur. That is far from the truth. I think a distinction should be drawn between credulity and credibility. Credulity is another word for gullibility, meaning that a person is willing to swallow almost anything. Credulous people leave their brains (and even authentic faith) at the door. Credulity opens one to being conned by hucksters and charlatans. The Church never asks us to be credulous.

Credibility has to do with believability. The apostles in

the resurrection stories of the Gospels were surely not credulous. They needed credibility. They had to be dragged kicking and screaming into really believing the Resurrection of Jesus. Even when they experienced appearances of the risen Christ, they drew back and exclaimed, "It is a ghost!" Jesus made his appearance credible by asking them to touch him, to give him something to eat.

Discerning the reality of Mary's appearances is a duty of the Church so that our faith may be enhanced and strengthened. It is not an exercise designed to make us skeptics. I believe with millions of others that Mary has appeared many times in Catholic history, that she is appearing today and doubtless will do so again in the future. I also believe we need the Church's guidance to help us determine where she has actually appeared.

Reflection

The rosary. "The Rosary takes its inspiration from the Gospel to suggest the attitude with which the faithful should recite it" (Pope Paul VI, *Marialis Cultus*).

Many of the appearances of Mary, especially at Fatima, have been associated with the praying of the rosary. Numerous popes and saints have urged the faithful to pray the rosary. In June 1987, Pope John Paul II, by way of satellite telecast, led the whole world in praying the rosary. Opening the Marian Year, this was a global prayer for peace offered by mass audiences at Marian shrines such as in Washington, D.C., Lourdes, Frankfurt, Manila, Bombay, Rio de Janeiro and Dakar in Africa.

When the pope survived the assassin's bullet in May 1981, he attributed this to Mary's intercession and expressed his gratitude by way of the rosary. His first public appearance after the assassination attempt was on October 7, 1981, the feast of the Holy Rosary. He noted that the bullet struck him on May 13, the anniversary of Mary's first appearance at Fatima in 1917.

He said he was "indebted to the Blessed Virgin. In
everything that happened to me on that very day, I felt
that extraordinary motherly protection and care, which
turned out to be stronger than the deadly bullet. Today
is the memorial of Our Lady of the Holy Rosary...I want
these first words that I address to you to be words of
gratitude, love and deep trust, just as the holy Rosary is
and always remains a prayer of gratitude, love and
trustful request: the prayer of the Mother of the Church.
I...invite you all to this prayer."
    —*Quoted in Thomas A. Thompson, S.M., and Jack*
    Wintz, O.F.M.,"The Rosary: A Gospel Prayer,"
    St. Anthony Messenger

The popularity of the rosary has been attributed to Saint
Dominic and the members of the Dominican Order. As a
prayer, its form developed slowly from the twelfth century
up to the fifteenth century. Apparently it grew out of the
laity's desire to have 150 prayers to match the 150 psalms
chanted by the monks and canons in monasteries and
cathedrals. In 1569, Pope Pius V officially recommended
the prayer "of 150 angelic salutations...with the Lord's
prayer at each decade...while meditating on the mysteries
which recall the entire life of our Lord Jesus Christ." This
Pope added the second part to the Hail Mary, and this form
of the prayer was eventually adopted for the rosary.

The rosary is a Scripture-based prayer. It begins with
the Apostles Creed, which is itself a summary of the great
mysteries of Catholic faith, based on Scripture, from creation through redemption and up to the resurrection of the
body and everlasting life. The Our Father which introduces
each mystery is taken from the Gospels. The first part of the
Hail Mary is composed from verses from the Gospel of
Luke (1:29 and 1:42)—the angel's words announcing
Christ's birth and Elizabeth's greeting to Mary.

The mysteries of the rosary center on the events of
Christ's life. The joyful mysteries deal with the Incarnation;
the sorrowful mysteries meditate on Christ's suffering and
death; the glorious mysteries contemplate his Resurrection,

Ascension and sending of the Spirit, as well as Mary's participation in his Resurrection by her Assumption and Crowning.

The repetition of the ten Hail Marys with each mystery is meant to lead us to restful and contemplative prayer related to the mystery. Many who say the rosary think of the words as background music that leads them to rest in the divine presence. The gentle murmur of the words brings them to the inner, silent center where Jesus' spirit dwells as in a temple.

I would think that most of the readers of this book know how to pray the rosary, but I suspect there are some who do not. So, if I may offer a public service here, I would like to outline the basics for reciting it. Normally a rosary is five decades, though you could do all fifteen if you wished. For those who know how to pray the rosary, obviously you can skip this section of the book. But you may find it helpful for friends of yours who haven't a clue on how to pray the rosary.

The rosary starts with the Apostles Creed.

> I believe in God, the Father almighty, the creator of heaven and earth. I believe in Jesus Christ, his only Son, our Lord. He was conceived by the Holy Spirit and born of the Virgin Mary. He suffered under Pontius Pilate, was crucified, died and was buried. He descended into hell. The third day he rose again. He ascended into heaven, and is seated at the right hand of the Father. He will come again to judge the living and the dead. I believe in the Holy Spirit, the holy Catholic Church, the communion of saints, the forgiveness of sins, the resurrection of the body, and life everlasting. Amen.

This is followed by one Our Father, three Hail Marys and a Glory be to the Father, and so on. You will see a bead by itself—right after the cross—for the Creed and Our Father. Hold this bead while saying those prayers. Then move to the three following beads for the Hail Marys. The next single bead is for the Glory be to the Father.

Now the five mysteries begin. For example, if you are praying the Joyful Mysteries, say, "First mystery, the Annunciation." You are holding what is usually a larger bead, or one by itself. While still holding this bead, say the Our Father. Then move on to the ten Hail Marys, moving your fingers to one bead at a time. Then you come to the next single bead and say the Glory be to the Father.

Stay there while you say, "Second Mystery, the Visitation, Our Father..." Then the Hail Marys and Glory Be as before. Repeat the process for the ensuing mysteries.

At the end of the rosary, it is customary to say the following prayers:

> Hail, Holy Queen, mother of mercy, our life, our sweetness and our hope. To you do we cry, poor banished children of Eve. To you do we send up our sighs, mourning and weeping in this valley of tears. Turn then, most gracious advocate, your eyes of mercy toward us and after this, our exile, show unto us the blessed fruit of your womb, Jesus. O clement, O loving, O sweet Virgin Mary.

> Pray for us, O holy mother of God.
> That we may be made worthy of the promises
> of Christ.

> Let us pray:
> O God, whose only begotten Son, by his life, death and resurrection, has purchased for us the rewards of eternal life, grant, we beseech you, that meditating on these mysteries of the most Holy rosary of the Blessed Virgin Mary, we may imitate what they contain and obtain what they promise, through the same Christ, our Lord. Amen.

Meditating on the mysteries of the rosary. *The Catechism of the Catholic Church,* 2708, offers these thoughts about meditating on Christ's mysteries:

Meditation engages thought, imagination, emotion and desire. This mobilization of faculties is necessary in order to deepen our convictions of faith, prompt the conversion of our heart and strengthen our will to follow Christ. Christian prayer tries above all to meditate on the mysteries of Christ, as in the lectio divina or the rosary. This form of prayerful reflection is of great value, but Christian prayer should go further: to the knowledge of the love of the Lord Jesus, to union with him.

Here are the titles of the fifteen mysteries of the rosary. You may want to read a passage from the Gospels as you recite each mystery.

Joyful Mysteries:
Annunciation
Visitation
Birth of Christ
Presentation of the Lord in the Temple
Finding of the young Christ in the Temple

Sorrowful Mysteries:
The Agony in the Garden
The Scourging at the Pillar
The Crowning With Thorns
The Carrying of the Cross
The Crucifixion

Glorious Mysteries:
The Resurrection
The Ascension
The Descent of the Holy Spirit
The Glorious Assumption of Mary
The Crowning of Mary

"In praying the Rosary with devotion, we are reliving the life of Christ" (Mother Teresa of Calcutta).

William Hart McNichols, S.J.
OUR LADY OF THE APOCALYPSE
1996
Private collection

CHAPTER TEN

❖

Mother of the Church

We proclaim the most holy Mary
as Mother of the Church.

—*Pope Paul VI, Discourse,*
November 21, 1964

I Felt a Mother's Love Had Touched Me

A retreat master was giving a retreat. Toward the end of it, a girl handed him a note. He put it in his pocket and forgot about it. After the retreat he found it, unfolded it, and read:

For the past eight months I have been in psychotherapy.

As a child I experienced overwhelming fear because of hatred and abuse. A major focus of my life right now is to overcome and transform that fear. The details are unnecessary, but much of my fear is centered on my mother.... I had become so turned off to the concept of mothers that I consciously rejected the love...of Mary, the mother of Jesus.

After your talk, I walked outside—feeling terribly alone. I prayed for the grace to break through the wall that was keeping me from trusting.... I wanted to cry, but haven't in months.

You may have noticed a small, round building near the cemetery. Curiosity is one of my strongest traits—I walked to it and opened the door.

When I looked inside, I was filled with fear. There stood a large statue of Mary. My first impulse was to run away in anger. But something drew me slowly to the kneeler at her feet. Then I fell to my knees, weeping into the folds of her robes.

When it was over, I felt cleansed and new. I felt willing to be a trusting child. Even more important, I felt that a mother's love had touched me, leaving in me a true desire to forgive my natural mother.

—*Quoted by Father Mark Link, S.J.,*
 in homily for Feast of Mother of God, Year C.

Unique in one way but universal in another, this young woman's story has been repeated thousands of times. The details of her journey are hers alone. The essence of it she shares with many others. Numberless lost souls have come to Mary and found the hope needed to start again. They found a spiritual mother in Mary.

They prayed for the grace to go through the wall that kept them from trusting. They discovered that Mary was there to help them do it. In God's wonderful plan to save us from ourselves, he gave us Mary to open our hearts and teach us how to trust and forgive. In this way Mary brings us to Christ and the Church.

It is a happy coincidence that the confession chapel at the National Shrine of the Immaculate Conception in Washington, D.C., is called the chapel of Our Lady of Hope. The Sacrament of Reconciliation is our constant source of hope. No matter how much we have sinned, abandoned loved ones, betrayed those who trusted us or let people down, we can be healed and forgiven by God. Our Blessed Mother will warmly draw us to this grace of forgiveness especially when we mistakenly think that we have committed the unforgivable sin, whatever that may be.

Generally it is our natural mothers who communicate to us our sense of trust and hope. Sadly, there are cases when some mothers fail to do this, as our opening story reminds us. Our heavenly mother can supply what our earthly mother may not have been able to give us. Better yet, our Blessed Mother can help us forgive the parent who could not help us.

The tears shed by the girl into the robes of Mary were a gift from God. Such tears awaken one to possibilities of a new start in life. If any of you reading this wonder if you can get beyond what seems a dead end, take the following prayer of Saint Bernard and go to Mary and pour out your heart with each word:

> Remember, O most loving Virgin Mary, that never was it known that anyone who fled to your protection, implored your help, or sought your intercession was left unaided. Inspired with this confidence, I turn to you, Virgin of virgins, my Mother. To you I come. Before you I stand, sinful and sorrowful. O Mother of the Word Incarnate, do not turn away from me, but in your mercy, hear and answer me. Amen.

Mary in the Mystery of the Church

At the beginning of the Third Session of Vatican II, Pope Paul VI declared that Mary was Mother of the Church. This was a new title for her. The discussions during the Council centered on whether the teachings concerning Mary should be in a special document or included in the constitution on the Church.

The bishops decided that they should place it in *Lumen Gentium*, their document on the Church. After all, the Church visibly began at Pentecost and Mary was in the midst of the Church in that great scene. Mary's role in salvation history was always related to Christ. Now it needed to be just as clear that Mary bears an essential relationship to the Church.

In this book I have tried to show that in our efforts to understand Jesus, we needed to turn to Mary. When the Gnostics denied Jesus was human, we argued he certainly was human, for he had a human mother from whose bone and blood he was born.

When Nestorius denied Mary was mother of God, the Church responded that the Son of God united to himself the humanity that Mary conceived. Jesus Christ was always God (and man) and Mary conceived him as such. In other words, when the Church affirmed that Jesus was divine from the beginning of his existence, it examined the nature of Mary's motherhood.

At Vatican II, the bishops also wanted us to see that Mary helps us understand the meaning of the Church.

> Through the gift of divine motherhood, Mary is united with her Son, the Redeemer, and with his singular graces and offices. By these the Blessed Virgin is also united with the Church: The Mother of God is a figure of the Church in the matter of faith, charity and perfect union with Christ.
> —*"The Church"*

The Council says that Mary is a "figure" of the Church. This is a poetic term meant to show there is an intimate parallel between Mary and the Church. For example, Mary is both mother and virgin. She is mother of Jesus and always a virgin for the purpose of giving an undivided heart to God.

Church as Mother

Like Mary, the Church has a maternal role. Even from apostolic times the Church understood this. "My little children, for whom I am again in the pain of childbirth until Christ is formed in you" (Galatians 4:19). The Church serves the world as a mother giving birth to people in Christ. The Church can never cease to look at Mary who gave birth to Christ himself. She is the original Christ-bearer. The Church contemplates Mary's maternal role in order to fulfill its own calling.

The Church learns "mothering" by looking in faith at the mystery of Mary "the Mother." This vision assists the Church to appreciate its vocation to be a sacrament of salvation for the world. Just as Mary, by the power of the Spirit, gave birth to the Christ, so the Church generates new sons and daughters of God by the power of the Spirit in Baptism and continues to nurture them in the other sacraments.

Church as Virgin

Secondly, Mary the virgin is a figure of the Church as virgin. "The Church herself is a virgin, who keeps whole and pure the fidelity she has pledged to her spouse" ("The Church"). The Church is the spouse of Christ. When Paul speaks to the Church of Corinth he uses wedding imagery. "I promised you in marriage to one husband, to present you as a chaste virgin to Christ" (2 Corinthians 11:2). Mary married Joseph, but remained a virgin. The Church married Christ and remains virginal.

The Council identifies virginity with a pure and chaste fidelity. This is the ideal Mary achieved by God's grace.

This is an ideal the Church must attain with the Spirit's power. This does not mean that every member of the Church must be technically a virgin—though many will be called to this state. The term *virgin* is applied here in the spiritual meaning of an undivided heart, of fidelity in its most luminous form. God calls the Church and all its members to fidelity to the union of love begun in Baptism and continued in the other sacraments.

Such fidelity includes a commitment to the teachings of the faith. Mary pondered in her heart the teachings of her Son. The Church, too, is called to retain, contemplate and probe the teachings of Christ. Virginal fidelity includes a commitment to faith and a lifelong growth in understanding and witnessing this faith.

Behold Your Mother

Mary is more than a model for the Church's maternal and virginal role. By her maternal mediation for us, Mary is also the Mother of the Church.

> For, "with maternal love she cooperates in the birth and development" of the sons and daughters of Mother Church. The Church's motherhood is accomplished not only according to the model and figure of the Mother of God, but also with her "cooperation." The Church draws abundantly from this cooperation, that is to say from the maternal mediation, which is characteristic of Mary.
> —*"Mother of the Redeemer"*

This is the real meaning of Christ's words to his mother at the Cross, "Woman, behold, your son" (John 19:26). These words determined Mary's place among the disciples. Jesus appoints Mary as a spiritual mother. It happens within the Paschal Mystery. Jesus has reached the summit of what he came to do, to die and rise for our salvation from sin and the gift of divine life. Mary received her new calling to spiritual motherhood in the environment of death and resurrection.

In John's Gospel, where her calling occurs, Jesus is lifted up on the cross and lifted up to glory. John's mystical insight shows Easter already embedded in the cross. Jesus makes Mary our spiritual mother precisely during the actual unfolding of the Paschal Mystery. Jesus establishes Mary as a mother in the order of grace. She will implore the Spirit to raise up new children redeemed by the sacrifice of Christ. It is the Son of God himself who has commissioned Mary to accept this vocation of spiritual mother of the Church by her cooperation with the Spirit and her intercessory mediation.

Mary Guides Us to Eucharist

The Church's faith in both East and West has always sensed Mary's close connection with the Eucharist. Drawn into the Paschal Mystery at Calvary and Easter by the will of Christ, Mary could want nothing more than to guide us to the table of the Eucharist.

All the approved modern apparitions of Mary result in a shrine church where millions of pilgrims celebrate the Eucharist and benefit from the salvation from sin and gift of divine life which Christ imparts. If Mary attracts people to the site of the appearance, it is only to implant the pilgrims into the mystery of Christ in the Eucharist.

How often she tells the seers, "Build a church here"— not just the building, but the Body of Christ where Eucharist is celebrated. For it is the Body of Christ in the Eucharist who builds the Body of Christ which is Mother Church.

The most noticeable fact about all true shrines of Mary is the conversion of millions at the confessional and the nurturing of them with the Bread of Life. Mothers feed their children. This great Mother gently nudges us to the altar of God to let Jesus feed them with his very Body and Blood. As medieval poets loved to say, "Mary is the moon who asks us to go to the sun with its warmth, light and life, her Son, the savior."

What Is a Mother?

> Of the essence of motherhood is the fact that it concerns
> the person. Motherhood always establishes a unique
> and unrepeatable relationship between two people:
> between mother and child and between child and
> mother. Even when the same woman is the mother of
> many children, her personal relationship with each one
> of them is of the very essence of motherhood. For each
> child is generated in a unique and unrepeatable way,
> and this is true both for the mother and child. Each
> child is surrounded in the same way by that maternal
> love on which are based the child's development and
> coming to maturity as a human being.
> —*"Mother of the Redeemer"*

The ideal mother has the capacity to relate to each of her
children in a singular and unique manner. This ideal
mother also has the ability to do this even when she has
many children. Pope John Paul II sees in this ideal of
earthly motherhood a comparison to Mary's maternal role
in the Church. He notes that Jesus commissions Mary to behold the apostle John as her son, a singular invitation, but
meant to apply to each one whom Christ will entrust to her
spiritual care.

Seen with the perspective of faith, it is not only John
who stood at the Cross, but every true disciple of Christ.
We all stand there and receive from the Redeemer our spiritual Mother, Mary. This was Christ's parting gift to each of
us just before his death and resurrection. Jesus made a personal gift of his mother to us. Jesus entrusted humanity to
Mary.

The Disciple Should Welcome the Mother

There is another aspect to this lovely scene. Jesus said to
John, "Behold, your mother" (John 19:27). Jesus had given
John a spiritual mother. Jesus also knew that Mary would
need someone to care for her now that he would be gone.

He entrusted his mother to the care of John. "And from that hour the disciple took her into his home" (John 19:27).

It is one thing for a Christian disciple to know that Mary is offered to him or her as a spiritual mother. The next step is to welcome her into one's home. We need to invite Mary into our homes and hearts. Mary is more than John's houseguest. Mary becomes a presence in his inner life. Mary must become a presence in our inner lives as well. The mystery of Mary affected the interior life of John in a positive and productive way. She can do the same for us once we have welcomed her into the privacy of our souls.

What does she tell you and me when we invite her into our home? She says, "Do whatever he tells you" (John 2:5). She points us to Jesus and asks us to be his disciple. She wants us to realize that Jesus is the one mediator between the Father and ourselves. He is "the way, the truth and the life" (John 14:6). Mary is so identified with Jesus that Dante has Bernard say, "Look now upon the face that most resembles Christ, for only through its brightness can you prepare your vision to see him" (*Paradiso*).

Our dear mother has "the face that most resembles Christ." Love becomes like the beloved. That is what Mary did in her life. When we welcome her into our awareness, she wants to do that for us. She wants our face to resemble Christ's. Is it not our goal to be Christlike? One of the wrinkliest faces on earth was the deeply lined countenance of Mother Teresa. Yet who could fail to see the beauty of Christ shining through her face? Creams hide wrinkles. But care-worn lines do not conceal the presence of Christ in the face of a person who loves him absolutely.

The Woman Accompanies the Saving Plan

When Vatican II placed Mary within the context of the Church, it clarified the biblical theme of the "Woman." God connects the woman with the plan of salvation, first in Genesis, then in the Gospels and finally in the Apocalypse. The biblical mystery of the woman begins and ends the story of salvation. After the Fall, God immediately promises hope and redemption. God speaks to the serpent, the source of the evil temptation:

> I will put enmity between you and the woman, and between your offspring and hers; he will strike your head, and you will strike his heel.
> —Genesis 3:15

The language is battle talk, violent, ringing with the struggle between good and evil. The verses lay out the reality of history as it will be experienced. Morality and immorality will fight for the human soul. Evil will bite the human heel. The Greek myth of the mighty Achilles reminds us that we are vulnerable to evil and its destructive force. We could lose the war.

But God has resolved to save us if we cooperate with him. The savior will destroy the head of the serpent whose teeth could open our bodies and fill us with poison. The savior will crush the head and source of evil.

Essential to this process is the role of the woman. Genesis does not specify who she is. The text speaks generally—the offspring of some woman will overcome evil. Who is she? Who will be involved in this monumental struggle? Centuries will pass before we know. Not until an angel appears to Mary and invites her to be the mother of the Savior do we know the identity of the woman. In John's Gospel, Jesus calls Mary "woman" two times—at Cana which marks the beginning of his saving mission, and at Calvary when Jesus accomplishes this mission. Mary is more than a stage prop at these two events. The "woman" initiates the process of Christ's saving mission. Then the "woman" offers her son to the Father at the Cross. She surrenders her physical maternity and receives a spiritual maternity instead and becomes Mother of the Church. The meaning of the woman in Genesis is clarified.

But the illumination of the biblical woman has one more unfolding. Mary's ecclesial identification reaches a summit in the Apocalypse where the "woman" appears clothed with the sun, standing on the darkness and ready to give birth to the savior who will strike a fatal blow at the head of the dragon/serpent who hopes to bite the savior's heel. It now becomes evident that the woman is not just Mary, but also the Church, Christ's instrument of salvation in the world. And Mary stands as the first true fulfillment of what the Church is meant to be. Who then is the woman of Genesis? The Gospels tell us it is Mary. Apocalypse tells us more; the woman is also the Church. Mary shows us what the Church is meant to be.

> But while in the most Blessed Virgin, the Church has already reached that perfection whereby she exists without spot or wrinkle (cf. Ephesians 5:27), the faithful still strive to conquer sin and increase in holiness.
> —*"The Church"*

We, the faithful, gaze on the mystery of Mary who helps us find in Christ the path to the Father. The Church embraces Mary, thus linking past, present and future in the process of salvation. As members of the Church we venerate Mary as our spiritual mother and advocate. Mary loves us. I ask you to join me in loving her. You will never regret it.

Reflection

We now conclude these meditations on Mary. I have asked you to dwell on ten images of our Blessed Mother. These are some of what Saint Alphonsus would call the "glories of Mary." No one image tells the whole story. God has adorned her with so many treasures that it takes whole libraries to tell her story.

Mary does not ask us to concentrate on her, but rather on Jesus and the Church. She called herself the "handmaid" of the Lord. The handmaid's eyes are not on herself, but on her Lord. Mary is a mirror of Christ and the Church.

She says, "When you look at me in faith, you will see

your savior Jesus and the Church which is his sacrament of salvation. I will gently turn your attention to your goal and destiny in God. I am your spiritual mother who will listen to your needs and bring them to my Son. I am not self-absorbed. I will help you to transcend yourself so you can find true human fulfillment, which can only happen with grace and a loving union with God. Because I love you with a mother's love, I will do this for you. I can do it because my Son makes it possible for me to assist you. Yes, I love you."

✳ *As I review the images of Mary, which ones touch me most and why are they so effective in my life?*

✳ *In these meditations, how have I grown in my appreciation of Mary's role in salvation and in my life? What is the enduring treasure I have drawn from my reflections on Mary?*

✳ *Among my friends and acquaintances, who best shows me how Mary has guided them to Christ and the Church and so has proved to be a blessing for their lives? What can I learn from their stories?*

✳ *If I compare my childhood love of Mary with where it is today, what do I see? Is my adult relationship with Mary better than it was in my youth? How would I evaluate my progress in this regard?*

✳ *What are areas of my relationship with Mary where I could improve?*

✳ *As a result of my reflections on Mary, what resolutions will I write out and practice?*

Prayer

We fly to your protection,
O holy Mother of God.
Despise not our petitions in our necessities,
But deliver us always from all dangers,
O glorious and blessed Virgin.

Ave Maria.

PERMISSIONS